THE BUMPS ARE
WHAT YOU CLIMB ON

THE BUMPS ARE WHAT YOU CLIMB ON

ENCOURAGEMENT FOR DIFFICULT DAYS

Warren Wiersbe

Inter-Varsity Press

INTER-VARSITY PRESS
38 De Montfort Street, Leicester LE1 7GP, England

First published in 1980

First British edition 1986
Reprinted 1987

These meditations were adapted from messages given by Dr Wiersbe on the radio programme, *Songs in the Night*

British Library Cataloguing in Publication Data

Wiersbe, Warren
    The bumps are what you climb on:
    encouragement for difficult days.
    1. Christian life
    I. Title
    248.4   BV4647.E5

UK ISBN 0-85110-486-X

Printed in Great Britain by Cox & Wyman Ltd, Cardiff Road, Reading

Inter-Varsity Press, England, is the publishing division of the Universities and Colleges Christian Fellowship (formerly the Inter-Varsity Fellowship), a student movement linking Christian Unions in universities and colleges throughout the United Kingdom and the Republic of Ireland, and a member movement of the International Fellowship of Evangelical Students. For information about local and national activities write to UCCF, 38 De Montfort Street, Leicester LE1 7GP.

Contents

Preface

We all need a word of encouragement from the Lord during these difficult days. And we all need to *share* that word of encouragement with others.

The emphasis in these brief messages is on *encouragement*. It is my prayer that these meditations will strengthen your heart, build your faith, increase your love, and make the blessed hope of our Lord's return shine even brighter.

These messages were first given over "Songs in the Night," the worldwide radio ministry of the Moody Church in Chicago. It was my privilege to serve as Senior Minister there for seven years and to be the regular radio speaker over this weekly broadcast.

Except for some minor revisions, these messages are printed here just as they were used over the air. This accounts for the informal style and for some occasional repetitions.

I trust that God's Word will encourage your heart, and that you, in turn, will encourage somebody else.

Warren W. Wiersbe

1

The Bumps Are
What You Climb On

A little boy was leading his sister up a mountain path and the way was not too easy. "Why, this isn't a path at all," the little girl complained. "It's all rocky and bumpy." And her brother replied, "Sure, the bumps are what you climb on." That's a remarkable piece of philosophy. What do you do with the bumps on the path of life?

I have been a reader of biographies for many years, and I have yet to find a successful person whose life was free from problems and difficulties. Looking at these people from a distance, you might think they had it made and that life was easy for them. But when you get closer, you discover that their climb to the top of the mountain was not an easy one. The road was rocky and bumpy, but the bumps were what they climbed on to get to the top.

We don't have to read too far in the Bible before we discover this truth. Abraham certainly didn't become a great man of faith overnight. He had to go through some difficult tests on the road of life before he reached the top of the mountain. No sooner did Abraham arrive in Canaan than a famine came to the land. Imagine facing a famine in the land God has promised you! Then Abraham had problems with his nephew, Lot; and then war came to the land, and Abraham had to go out and fight. His wife led him astray with bad counsel and the result was the birth of Ishmael, a boy who brought sorrow to Abraham's heart. Finally, Isaac, the promised son, was born, bringing great joy to Abraham and Sarah. Then God asked Abraham to put Isaac on the altar, a sacrifice that would be difficult for any father or mother. Yes, there were many bumps on that road, but Abraham used the bumps to climb higher.

If anybody walked a rocky road, Joseph did. He was pampered by his father, hated by his brothers, sold for a slave, falsely accused, put into prison, forgotten, and apparently forsaken. But the bumps on the road helped him to climb higher, and one day Joseph became the second in command of all Egypt. Moses had a similar experience, and so did David, Daniel, and Paul. Here were people who did not complain about the road; they accepted the difficulties of life and used them as stepping-stones to the top of the mountain.

I don't know what difficulties you are going through just now, but I know some of the feelings you have, because I have been on this bumpy road myself. You feel like quitting, like giving up. You can't understand why the road doesn't get easier, why God doesn't remove the stones and straighten the path. If God did that, you might never get to the top, because the bumps are what you can climb on.

Psalm 91 says, "He that dwelleth in the secret place of the Most High shall abide under the shadow of the Almighty." It is a psalm that magnifies the care that God exercises over His children. Eleven different kinds of dangers are named in this psalm—war, snares, sickness, terrors by night, arrows by day, and others—yet God says that He can protect us from them all. This doesn't mean that we will never experience accidents or injuries; but it does mean that no matter what happens in the will of God, all things will work together for good.

One of the greatest promises found in Psalm 91 has to do with the stones on the path. "For he shall give his angels charge over thee, to keep thee in all thy ways. They shall bear thee up in their hands, lest thou dash thy foot against a stone." God doesn't promise to remove the stones from the path, but He does promise to make them stepping-stones and not stumbling blocks. He promises to help us climb higher because of the difficulties of life.

Most of us respond in a predictable way to the rocks in the path. We complain about them; we kick against them and only hurt ourselves. We try to pick them up and get rid of them, only to discover they are too heavy for us. We can't always get around them, and we wonder if we can get over them. Some people just stop and go no further. Others give up and turn back. But the child of God does not have to stop or go back; he can use the rocky places in life as stepping-stones to climb higher.

The trouble with most of us is that we are accustomed to paved roads and level sidewalks. But life is not made that way. Sometimes the road is level and easy, and the birds are singing and the way is wonderful. But sometimes the road is rocky and bumpy, and we hear no music and feel no helping hand. Then what? Complain? Give up? No, that's the time to remember God's promise: "For he shall give his angels charge over thee to keep thee in all thy ways." God's invisible army is at your service, and God can see you through.

Charlie Brown in the "Peanuts" comic strip is one of my favorite characters. In one particular strip, he is complaining because his team always loses their games. Lucy tries to console him by saying, "Remember, Charlie Brown, you learn more from your defeats than you do from your victories," And Charlie Brown replies, "That makes me the smartest man in the world!"

If life were nothing but a series of defeats, all of us would get discouraged. God knows how to balance our lives so that we have sunshine and rain, calm and storm, laughter and tears. On the road of life there are level places that delight us, and there are difficult places that challenge us. If we get off the path of God's will and go on a detour, the way will be rough from start to finish. The detour is always rougher than the main road. But there are rocks and bumps even on the paths of God's choosing, and we have to learn to accept them and benefit from them. The bumps are what you climb on.

But this takes faith. It is much easier to kick the rock and turn around and go back. The secret to climbing higher is to look away from yourself and your difficulties, and look by faith to Jesus Christ. He knows where you are, how you feel, and what you can do. Turn it all over to Him and start walking by faith. The very rocks that seem like barriers to human eyes will, to the eyes of faith, become blessings. Listen to the promises of Psalm 91:15: "He shall call upon me, and I will answer him: I will be with him in trouble; I will deliver him and honor him."

If anybody faced obstacles on the road of life, it was our Lord Jesus Christ. He was born into a poor family, a member of a rejected minority race. He grew up in obscurity in a little town that was mentioned only in scorn—"Can any good thing come out of Nazareth?" He gathered about Him a small group of nondescript men, and one of them became a traitor and sold Him for the price of a slave. He was called a liar, a glutton, a drunkard, a man in league with the devil. Men twisted His words and questioned His motives, yet Jesus Christ continued to do the will of God. Finally, He came to that greatest stone of all—being crucified like a common thief. But He continued to climb that mountain, and God gave Him the victory.

This is why the writer of the Book of Hebrews urges us to look to Jesus Christ and keep on trusting. "Looking unto Jesus the author and finisher of our faith, who for the joy that was set before him, endured the cross, despising the shame, and is set down at the right hand of the throne of God." We are to look not at ourselves, our circumstances, our troubles, or the bumps in the road, but unto Jesus. Yes, the bumps are what you climb on!

2

God Reigns

God is on the throne! The apostle John speaks this word of encouragement forcefully in Revelation 19:6: "Allelujah: for the Lord God omnipotent reigneth!"

Sometimes it looks as though the throne of the universe is empty. We see violence and crime and don't always see the justice that is supposed to follow. We see lies prosper while truth fades, and evil seems to be in control of the world God made. Sometimes we wonder if it is really worth it to trust Christ and try to be obedient to Him.

The apostle John lived in a world not too different from ours. Of course, when he wrote the Book of Revelation, he wasn't sitting in a comfortable church study or college library surrounded by books and admiring students. No, when John wrote the Revelation, he was a prisoner of Rome, exiled on the Isle of Patmos, surrounded by the waters of the Aegean Sea and separated from the people he loved. Imagine if you will this old man who had faithfully served Christ, now alone in exile, suffering for his faith. And yet, when he writes a book, it is not about himself and his trials; it is about Jesus Christ and His triumphs. He doesn't write, "Woe is me, Caesar is on the throne." That's not the language of faith! No, John writes, "Allelujah: for the Lord God omnipotent reigneth!"

It may seem that the throne of the universe is empty, but it isn't. God is still on the throne. And He is the *Lord* God. Yearly every Roman citizen had to appear at an altar dedicated to Caesar, drop in a pinch of incense, and say, "Caesar is Lord." John wouldn't do that. He stood up and boldly said, "Jesus Christ is Lord!" Thus they arrested him and put him in exile. But John didn't see himself as the prisoner of Caesar; he was the prisoner of Jesus Christ! And he wasn't suffering; he was sharing in the *glory* of Christ! No matter how dark the day, no matter how heavy the burden, John was able to look up and say, "Allelujah: for the Lord God omnipotent reigneth!"

God is reigning today. He has not abdicated his throne and turned the universe over to the enemy. It is true that much that goes on in this world is contrary to His will; but where He does not rule, He overrules, and His purposes are going to be fulfilled. After all, He is the Lord—the God omnipotent, all powerful.

We can entrust our lives and our loved ones into the hands of this kind of God. When you find yourself discouraged or worried or afraid, just remember that "The Lord God omnipotent reigneth." This is the secret of peace and joy in the midst of a troubled world. This is how the prophet Isaiah found strength when his world fell apart. The nation of Judah was ruled by godly King Uzziah, a man who did wonders for his people. But one day, King Uzziah died; and Isaiah thought everything was going to end. He tells us about it in the sixth chapter of his prophecy: "In the year that King Uzziah died I saw also the Lord sitting upon a throne, high and lifted up, and his train filled the temple." What a sight that must have been! The throne on earth was empty, but the throne in heaven was filled. On earth, the people were mourning, but in heaven the seraphim were praising God and saying, "Holy, holy, holy, is the Lord of hosts: the whole earth is full of his glory!" This vision of the throne of God transformed young Isaiah; it made him a new man. Instead of sitting and complaining, Isaiah dedicated himself to God and went out and started witnessing.

The apostle Paul had a similar experience. It is recorded in the eighteenth chapter of Acts. Paul had come to the city of Corinth to preach and to establish a church, and the going was really tough. To begin with, Corinth was a very wicked city; and the opposition of the enemy was overwhelming. In fact, Paul must have felt like quitting. But one night, Jesus came to Paul and said, "Be not afraid, . . . for I am with thee . . . for I have much people in this city." Paul stayed in Corinth for a year and a half and built a witnessing church. What was it that made the difference? Paul discovered that God was still on the throne.

And, that's what you and I are going to have to discover if we are going to make it in this difficult world. We can't depend upon our own rule, because we are weak and ignorant. And we can't depend too much on the rule of others, because they are as weak and ignorant as we are. The only thing we can depend on is the rule and reign of Jesus Christ our Lord and Savior. If He is on the throne of our lives, then we can face tomorrow with courage and confidence.

I was chatting with a college student who was greatly concerned about the age-old problem of evil in the world. She couldn't understand why a God of love and power would permit such atrocities and evils to occur. Of course, I reminded her that mankind is reaping the results of rebellion against God. God is not to blame for the evil in the world; this is the result of sin. Furthermore, God has privileged man to have the power of choice, and man still makes the wrong choices.

But the biggest problem is not the presence of evil in this world, it's the presence of good! The fact that God has not poured out His judgments on mankind is, to me, a bigger problem than the evils we see men inflicting on each other! God is on the throne, and He has the power to judge this world right now, yet He restrains His wrath. This is not the day of judgment; this is the day of salvation. "The Lord God omnipotent reigneth," but He chooses today to reign in grace, and not in wrath.

The apostle Peter explains it clearly in the third chapter of his second letter. "The Lord is . . . long-suffering to usward, not willing that any should perish, but that all should come to repentance." Please don't get the idea that, because God has not judged the world's sin or your sin, He is not going to do it at all. Judgment day is coming, but right now God is being patient with sinners, lovingly and graciously inviting them to trust Christ and be saved. One of these hours, the day of grace will end and the day of wrath will begin, and then it will be too late. The throne of grace will become a throne of judgment and justice, and all who have never trusted Christ will be lost forever.

Have you ever humbled yourself before God's throne and yielded your life to Christ? He died in your place on the cross. He bore your sins. And He wants to forgive you, save you from judgment, and give you His eternal, abundant life. Are you really glad that Christ is reigning? Is He reigning over your life? If He is on the throne of your heart, then you can face the future with joy and say, "Allelujah, for the Lord God omnipotent reigneth!"

3

Three Important Looks

The last words of important people have always interested me. Napoleon's final words were, "France—army-head of army!" John Wilkes Booth, who shot President Lincoln, had two final words before he died: "Useless—useless." British naval hero Lord Nelson said, "Thank God I have done my duty." But among the greatest words of all are those written by the apostle Paul from a Roman prison: "For I am now ready to be offered, and the time of my departure is at hand. I have fought a good fight, I have finished my course, I have kept the faith: Henceforth there is laid up for me a crown of righteousness, which the Lord the righteous judge shall give me at that day: and not to me only, but unto all them also that love his appearing" (II Tim. 4:6-8).

As Paul awaited execution, he wrote a farewell letter to his dear comrade in service, Timothy. He wrote with assurance, not with fear and apprehension. There is a quiet confidence in his words. He knows that he faces death, but this does not frighten him. He knows that his work is almost over, but this does not discourage him. His words come with courage and calmness, and in this statement of faith, Paul looks in three directions and bears witness to his confidence in the Lord.

First, Paul *looks around* and bears witness that he is ready. What an amazing view of death! He does not look upon himself as a prisoner being executed, but as a sacrifice being offered to the glory of the Lord. His life is not being taken from him; he is offering his life to the Lord. After all, Jesus laid down his life for Paul, and the great apostle now lays down his life for his Savior.

In this statement, Paul avoids using the word *death*. It is not that he is afraid of the word, or even afraid of the experience. It is simply that, for the Christian, there is no such thing as death. The word Paul uses is *departure,* and what a beautiful word it is in the Greek language.

It means, for one thing, to take down your tent and move on, the way a soldier would do when the army strikes camp. Paul saw himself as one of God's soldiers, living in a tent— his mortal body. He knew that death was simply taking down the tent and moving into glorious new quarters. Our bodies are just temporary dwelling places. When the Lord calls us home, we will receive marvelous new bodies, permanent houses, and we will have them for all eternity.

The word *departure* also means to loose a boat and set sail. This is what happens when a Christian dies—he looses his moorings in this life and this world, and sets sail toward heaven and that eternal shore. Tennyson used this idea in his famous poem "Crossing the Bar." Paul knew that his death was simply a release. The prison was not his permanent home. His little ship would be loosed and he would arrive at the heavenly shore to meet the Lord Jesus Christ.

Can you look around with confidence as Paul did and know that you are ready to be offered? If you have trusted Christ as your Savior, then you are ready, and there is nothing to fear.

Paul not only *looked around* as he came to the end of his life; he also *looked back.* "I have fought a good fight, I have finished my course, I have kept the faith." Because he trusted Jesus Christ, Paul could look around without fear, and he could look back without regrets.

Many people try to avoid looking back. To be sure, there is a wrong way to look back; it is wrong to look back at past sins and failures and defeats. That can only make you fail even more today. But it is good to look back to see where we have been and what the Lord has done in us and through us.

As Paul looked back, he saw that life had not always been easy. There had been battles to fight, races to run, a stewardship to fulfill. He had fought the world, the flesh, and the devil in city after city, and now he was in his final battle at Rome. There were times when he thought he was going to fail, but the Lord had always brought him through. He could write, "I have fought a good fight."

He could also write, "I have finished my course." This had always been Paul's great desire: "That I might finish my course with joy and the ministry that God has given me. . . ." Each of us has a course to finish. God has a place for each of us to fill and a work for each of us to do. Our times are in His hands. Some are allotted a shorter span for their work; others are given more time. Stephen died as a young man; Paul was permitted to live a longer life. But it is not the length of life that counts—it is the depth and strength of life. Paul had finished his course. He could face the Lord and know that his work had been completed.

He had kept the faith. Even in Paul's day there were professed Christians who had departed from the faith. Paul warned Timothy, "This know also, that in the last days, some shall depart from the faith. . . ." The faith means "the faith once delivered to the saints," that body of saving truth that cost Jesus Christ His life and that is recorded in the Word of God. As a good steward, Paul had protected the faith in many a battle. He had invested it in many lives. Now he was going to pass off the scene.

Take time to look back. Have you fought a good fight? Are you a victor or a victim? Are you in the battle or a casualty on the field? Have you finished your course? Did you do the will of God from your heart? And have you kept the faith? Are you true to the teaching of the Word of God? Paul could look around without fear, and he could look back without regret. I trust that you and I can do the same.

Paul not only *looked around* and *looked back,* but he also *looked ahead.* "Henceforth there is laid up for me a crown of righteousness, which the Lord the righteous judge shall give me at that day; and not to me only, but unto all them also which love his appearing."

Some people, when they approach the end of life, are afraid to look ahead. The Bible warns us, "It is appointed unto men once to die, and after that the judgment." But Paul had no fears as he looked ahead. He knew just what would happen: he would meet the Lord and receive from the Lord the crown that he had earned.

There is no peace like the peace we have in our hearts when we know the future is secure. Paul's faith was not in Roman justice or law, as great as they might be. His faith was not in his many friends, or even in himself. His faith was in the Lord. He looked back without regret; he looked around without fear; and he looked ahead without doubt or apprehension because he trusted in Jesus Christ. Rome would register him as a criminal, but in the Lamb's Book of Life he would be listed as a child of God. And he would hear from his Savior, "Well done, thou good and faithful servant. . . ."

One day life is going to end for you and me. None of us knows the day or the hour, and for some it may be sooner than expected. Our home-going may be sudden; or we may have time to contemplate life as Paul did in that Roman prison. I trust that all of us will be able to look in these same three directions and come out with the same ringing testimony that Paul gives in this last letter that he ever wrote. Yield your heart and life to Jesus Christ. Be faithful to Him, no matter what men may do. The important thing is not the praise of men; it is the approval of God.

4

Never Forsaken

I like to begin each day by laying hold of some promise from God's Word that can guide and encourage me. The world changes—circumstances change, we change—but God's Word never changes. Let me share a great promise with you: Psalm 37:25 says, "I have been young, and now am old; yet have I not seen the righteous forsaken nor his seed begging bread." David wrote these words out of his own experience with life. When he became old he looked back and discovered how faithfully God had cared for him.

You and I may want to stop getting older, but there is really nothing we can do about it. I was watching several children running on the church steps one Sunday, and I said to one of the parents, "It's really a shame to waste all that energy on children!" How I wish I had more energy and more time to get more done. But life moves on, one day at a time, and we find ourselves getting older.

But getting older is a part of life. Paul tells us that the outward man is perishing, but the inward man is being renewed day by day. The body gets one day older, but the spirit becomes more like Christ—and we move one day closer to glory. Each stage of life has its burdens and its benefits. A child is free to play, and he has no burdens to carry, yet he is immature and really doesn't know what life is all about. A teenager has some adult privileges, but he has to start carrying some adult responsibilities. A single person has more freedom than a married person, yet most people would rather be married, even though marriage entails many extra burdens. Young people just getting started face so many unknowns in life; and middle-aged people sometimes get discouraged because they didn't reach all their goals.

Then we come to our senior years, when we would like to do so much more, yet we're hindered by physical handicaps, or perhaps by financial burdens. I'm not saying that life is just one big burden—not in the least! What I am saying is that life keeps moving along—we grow older—and each stage in life has its blessings and its burdens, its opportunities and its obligations. What David is saying is wonderful—*God is with us all the way.* When David was young, God was with him and helped him kill the giant. When David became old, God was still there and helped him stabilize the kingdom and prepare for the building of the temple. "I have been young, and now am old; yet have I not seen the righteous forsaken nor his seed begging bread." This is a heartening promise for the Christian believer. No matter how you may change or how life may change, God never changes, and His promises never fail.

When David grew to be an old man, he looked back at his stormy life and came to a wonderful conclusion—God had been with him all the way. God never forsakes His own. This truth is stated often in the Bible. Jesus said to His disciples before He returned to heaven, "Lo, I am with you always, even to the end of the age." You can be sure, my friend, that God is going to be with you. He will not forsake you.

As we review the life of David, we realize that he was not always walking in the will of God. There were days when he was discouraged and wanted to quit. Read the Psalms and you will discover that often David was defeated and living under the dark cloud of doubt, but God was still with him. When David was in the caves, hiding from King Saul, God was with him. Even when David doubted that God could help him, God was still there. God did not forsake David in those hours of defeat and discouragement.

But what about those hours of disobedience? Yes, there were times in David's life when he disobeyed God and sinned. Did God approve of that sin? Of course not! Did God deal with David's sin? Yes, He did. David was chastened for his disobedience. But did God forsake His child because he had sinned? No! There were times when David was not acceptable, but he was still accepted. David's salvation depended on the grace of God, not his own good works; and God was faithful to keep His promise. God had to rebuke and discipline David, but God never forsook him.

The fact that God does chasten us when we refuse to confess our sins is proof that He is *with* us and not *against* us. As parents, we often have to spank our children, and we do it because we love them. When a child disobeys, he doesn't cease being a member of the family! His fellowship with the family may be broken, but his sonship goes right on. We don't forsake our children when they disobey, and God the heavenly Father doesn't forsake us when we sin. He lovingly warns us, convicts us, rebukes us, and, if necessary, chastens us; and all of this is proof that He has not forsaken us.

Perhaps you feel that you have disobeyed God, and have been forsaken. Claim the promise of Psalm 37:25: "I have been young, and now am old; yet have I not seen the righteous forsaken nor his seed begging bread." If God ever forsook you for an instant, you would die, for "in him we live and move and have our being." Rest on His promise. God *has not* forsaken you, and God *will not* forsake you.

The promise of Psalm 37:25 also assures us of *God's provision*—we never become beggars. David is saying: God will always provide whatever we need so that we don't have to turn to anyone else except Him.

Is God concerned about the everyday needs of your life? Of course He is! Jesus told us that God watches the sparrows when they fall, and surely God sees us and knows our needs.

As Jesus ministered here on earth during those three marvellous years, He met the physical, emotional, and material needs of people. He was concerned about the children; He had time for the lepers and the handicapped; He fed hungry people. Of course, His greatest deed was His death on the cross for the sins of the world, for man's greatest need is salvation. Jesus Christ was not deaf to the pleas of the blind; He heard the cries of the sorrowing; and He met the needs of the people.

God is still answering prayer. David looked back at his long, full life and concluded that God had never forsaken him, and that God had provided for every need—and always would. No matter what your circumstances are just now, if you know Christ as your Savior and are living for Him, you can be sure that He will meet your every need. "But seek ye first the kingdom of God and his righteousness, and all these things shall be added unto you."

David was right. In spite of his inconsistencies and failures in life, he was cared for by God in a gracious and wonderful way. Turn your life over to Christ, and one of these days you will be able to say with David, "I have been young, and now am old; yet have I not seen the righteous forsaken nor his seed begging bread."

5

Constant Care

A friend sent me the following simple and encouraging poem.

> Yesterday God helped me,
> Today He'll do the same.
> How long will this continue?
> Forever—praise His name!

—Yes, the same God who helped us yesterday and who is helping us today will go on helping us throughout all our tomorrows and into eternity. David wrote in Psalm 54:4, "Behold, God is mine helper!"

One problem we face as human beings is the malfunctioning of the memory. Too often we remember what we are supposed to forget, and we forget what we should remember! God says, "Your sins and your iniquities will I remember no more." Yet many Christians go through life shackled with the memory of sins God has already forgotten. Paul wrote, "Forgetting those things which are behind," and yet so many people I meet are still chained to the failures and mistakes of the past. Ask God to give you a poor memory when it comes to the sins of the past that God has already forgiven, buried, and forgotten.

But ask God to give you a good memory when it comes to the help He has given you in the past years of your life. For some reason, we forget the mercies and blessings of the past;

and for that reason, we get discouraged in the present and become fearful about the future. God has taken care of you up to this hour, *and He is never going to forsake you!*

Remembering God's help and care is the central theme of the Book of Deuteronomy. Moses is preparing the nation of Israel to go into the Promised Land. How does he do it? He reminds them that for forty years God has taken care of them and that God's care is not going to stop when they cross the river. Moses said, "Thou shalt remember all the way in which the Lord led you. . . ." You were hungry, and God gave you food. You were thirsty, and God gave you water. You were attacked by the enemy, and God gave you victory. You sinned, and God gave you forgiveness. There was no situation too hard for God.

A famous philosopher has said, "Those who do not know the past are condemned to repeat it." This is why Moses commanded the fathers in Israel to teach their children the Word of God and to remind their children of the great things God had done for the nation.

Yesterday God helped us, otherwise we would not be here. Like the prophet Samuel, we can erect a memorial to the faithfulness of God. Samuel called the memorial "Ebenezer—thus far the Lord has helped us." And like Abraham, we can look to the future and know that God will continue to help us. Abraham called the name of the memorial "Jehovah-Jireh—the Lord will see to it." So, you and I don't have to fret over the past or worry about the future, because God is our helper and He will never fail.

God's care for His own is not an occasional thing; it is constant. God is not like a physician who comes to us only when there is trouble. He is constantly walking with us and watching over us. When we go through the fire, He is there, as He was with the three Hebrew children in Babylon. When we go through the waters, He is there, as He was with the disciples in that storm on Galilee. Yes, even when we go through the valley of the shadow of death, He will be with us! "I will never leave thee nor forsake thee!" is His promise, and that promise is sure.

The enemy wants us to think that God doesn't care, or that God has forsaken us. When the going gets tough, the enemy says, "If God really loved you, this wouldn't have happened." How many times in pain or sorrow Satan has tried to cast doubts on the love and faithfulness of God. Somehow we have the idea that when life is *easy,* God is with us; but when life is *hard,* God has forsaken us—and just the opposite might be true. Too often when life is easy we forget God and start to depend on our own wisdom and strength. It is when the going is hard that we really know how close God is to His needy children.

It has wisely been said, "Never doubt in the darkness what God has told you in the light." The Bible makes it clear that God cares for His own. God doesn't promise us an easy path, but He does promise to help us and see us through. God won't remove the stones from the path, but He will command His angels to make sure we don't stumble over them. We are God's children, and our loving heavenly Father will never abandon us to the enemy. Even if our faith wavers, God will remain faithful, and His Word will never change.

Why does God help us? Is it because we deserve it? Of course not! If God gave us what we deserved, we would be in the darkness of judgment forever right now. God helps us because He loves us. Just as an earthly father cares for his children, so our heavenly Father cares for us. It is because of His grace that we have been saved. God has poured out upon us the riches of His grace and His love. We belong to Him, and He will never let us down.

Many people have the idea that the Christian life is something that starts with faith in Christ, but continues on the basis of our own efforts. But this is not true. We are *saved* by faith, and we *live* by faith. Surely if Christ could do the hardest thing possible—save our souls from judgment—then

He can do the easy things, like keeping us and providing for our daily needs.

Often my ministry takes me to other cities. Once I board a jet and get into my seat and fasten the seat-belt, I just relax and turn the whole trip over to God and the crew. I don't try to fly the plane. All of my worrying and fretting will never change one rivet or one bolt in that airplane. Life is like this. You have trusted Christ as your Savior, and you belong to Him. Just rest in Him. Don't try to fly the plane—just yield to Christ and let His loving care overshadow you.

After all, God cannot afford to fail us. If He fails, then everything in this universe falls to pieces. God must be true to Himself and true to His Word. God cannot lie. His promises are sure and steadfast. If God once failed to care for one of His children, *He* would lose far more than *we* would. His very character is at stake! He has promised to care for us, and if He doesn't keep His promise, then He has ceased to be God. You can be sure that this will never happen.

Those times when we thought God had failed us turned out to be times when He was working in a wonderful way on our behalf. Jacob thought that Joseph was dead, when all the time Joseph was preparing him a home in Egypt "All these things are against me!" mourned Jacob, when really everything was working together for his good.

> Yesterday God helped me,
> Today He'll do the same.
> How long will this continue?
> Forever—praise His name!

6

In Everything Give Thanks

Life has its perplexities and even its tragedies. Experiences come to us that we simply don't understand. In fact, there are times when it is very difficult to be thankful. Yet I Thessalonians 5:18 commands us, "In everything give thanks: for this is the will of God in Christ Jesus concerning you."

At this point you may say, "But there's a difference between giving thanks in everything and giving thanks *for* everything." I agree. But the Lord wants us to do both. I Thessalonians 5:18 commands me to give thanks in everything, and Ephesians 5:20 says, "Giving thanks always for all things. . . ." You cannot escape the fact that God expects us to be thankful no matter what circumstances may come to our lives.

These verses are easier read than obeyed. When I'm expected at a conference and my flight is cancelled because of weather, it is not easy to give thanks. When a valued officer in the church is transferred to another city and you don't have an immediate replacement, you find it hard to be thankful. When a loved one is sick or is taken in death, it is not easy to give thanks. Is God commanding the impossible? Is He mocking us and making the pain even worse? It is bad enough that we suffer because of the circumstances, but must we suffer guilt as well because we aren't really thankful?

Let's begin with an obvious fact: God *never* commands what He cannot enable us to fulfill, otherwise He would be mocking us and weakening His own Word. When Jesus was ministering on earth, His commandments enabled people to do the impossible. He commanded a man with a crippled hand to stretch out his hand, and the man did it and was healed. He commanded a paralytic to get up and walk, and the man did it. It has well been said that God's commandments are God's enablements. So, if God commands me to be thankful *for* all things and *in* all things, then He will enable me to obey Him, and I will be a better person because of it.

How does God give us this enablement? How are we able to wake up in the intensive care ward of the hospital and still give thanks? How can we stand by an open grave and give thanks and not be a hypocrite? The answer is found in those three great Christian virtues—faith, hope, and love. When faith, hope, and love are vital powers in our lives, then no matter what difficulties may come, we'll be able to thank our Father in heaven and bring glory to His name.

If you love somebody, you will not be afraid of him. The apostle John writes, "Perfect love casteth out fear," and this is true. I cannot conceive of a child loving a parent and then being deathly afraid of that parent, unless, of course, there is some kind of emotional instability. This is why faith and love go together: when you love somebody, you trust him—you are not afraid of him.

This relationship applies to the Christian and the Lord. If we love our Father in heaven, then we will not be afraid of what He may permit to come to our lives. If He loves us, He cannot harm us. He may permit suffering and sorrow, but He can never permit His child to be harmed by the trials of life. God permitted Job to go through all kinds of trials, yet in the end, the trials were for Job's good and God's glory. Job suffered, but his suffering led to glory. Job wept, but his tears were turned to joy. You can be sure that your Father in heaven loves you, and therefore He can be trusted.

Now let's apply this truth to some of the everyday difficulties of life. Some difficulty comes to us, perhaps a seeming tragedy. Our first reaction is, "Why did this happen?" Our second reaction is probably, "Why did this happen to *me*?" After all, if I am walking with the Lord, obeying Him, and serving Him, why should this trial come to my life?" If we aren't careful, at this point, the devil will come on the scene and start making matters worse. He is the accuser of the brethren and is skilled at getting us to doubt God's love and care. He will say, "If God loves you so much, why did this happen? I thought God promised to care for His children. He certainly isn't caring for you."

At this stage in your experience, lay hold of the truth that God loves you, and don't let anybody steal it away from you. Circumstances may assail you; Satan may accuse you; your Christian friends may even abandon you, but God loves you just as much as He did when He gave Jesus to die for you on the cross. Your circumstances have changed, and your feelings have changed, but God's love has not changed.

When you experience the love of God in your heart, then your faith will grow stronger, and you will be able to give thanks. To be sure, giving thanks when everything is falling apart is a real act of faith, but we Christians "walk by faith and not by sight." We say to ourselves, "My Father loves me and knows all about this difficulty. Because He loves me, I can trust Him. He has some wonderful purpose in mind that I cannot see just now. Though He slay me, yet will I trust Him." When you and I express out of faith and love like that, the Father will fill our hearts with His blessing and we will be able to give thanks. It is a miracle of God's grace, and it really works.

Love increases our faith, and when we have faith and love, we will have hope. Let me illustrate it with a child and his parents. The parents take the child to the doctor for his regular checkup, and the doctor discovers that the child needs surgery. Of course, the child is upset; he is sure that if his mother and father really love him, they will call the whole thing off. But the parents know what is best for their child, and the child knows he can trust his parents even when he doesn't agree with what is going on. Father says to the boy, "Now, after the surgery you'll have to stay in the hospital a few days; so Mother and I will visit you, and we'll do some fun things together. Then, when you get home, we have some exciting things planned." Because the boy loves his parents, and trusts them, he has something to look forward to—and that is hope.

When you and I go through the hardships of life, our heavenly Father says to us: "You don't understand all of this, but I do, and I know it is for your good. Trust me and be sure of my love. I have some wonderful things planned for you—not only in this life, but in the next life in glory, so don't be discouraged." Faith and love unite to produce hope, and when we have faith, hope, and love, we don't find it difficult to give thanks!

"In everything give thanks. . . ." We cannot obey that commandment in our own strength; we need the power of the Spirit of God and the encouragement of the Word of God. We look at the situation through tear-filled eyes and wonder what God has planned, but we know that His love can never fail us. Because we love Him and He loves us, we trust Him, and as our hope grows stronger, we are able to praise the Lord and give thanks—*in* everything and *for* everything.

7

Defeating Depression

In Psalms 42 and 43, three times we find the psalmist asking, "Why art thou cast down O my soul, and why art thou disquieted in me?" His world had fallen apart, and he was wondering where God was. He was wondering if he would ever get out of the dark pit of depression.

Depression is a serious problem in today's world. It is costing employers millions of dollars because their employees either are not on the job, or, if they are on the job, they are not productive. It is costing families their happiness, and in too many instances, depression is costing lives. Many people commit suicide in the vise of depression when all hope and all reason for living are squeezed out of them! Depression is a serious thing, and we must know how to handle it.

To be sure, depression sometimes has *a physical cause*. You will remember how discouraged the prophet Elijah was after his battle on Mt. Carmel. What he needed was some sleep, some good food, and a new vision of the greatness of God. Tenderly the Lord cared for Elijah, helped him rest and gain strength, and then the Lord recommissioned him for service. Many of us have had days of discouragement and despair because we have overworked, even in the service of the Lord! No wonder Jesus encouraged His disciples to come apart and rest awhile. If we are not careful, poor health habits can lead us into depression.

Sometimes depression is the result of *the attack of Satan*. He is the accuser and the destroyer. He knows when to attack us and what weapons to use. He likes to remind us of our failures and our past sins. He tries to get us to look at ourselves so much that we forget to look to Christ; and the result is almost always a feeling of guilt and failure and despair.

Some depression has *a psychological cause*. I am not a psychologist, so I cannot explain this in medical terms; but some people seem to have a personality that is naturally gloomy and pessimistic. Instead of trying to change this, they give in to it, and gradually they develop a pattern of defeat and depression. What they need is a competent Christian counselor to help them with their personality weaknesses.

I will not try to be either a doctor or a psychologist; I will simply be a pastor. I want to share with you some facts about depression that will help you when you find yourself in what John Bunyan called the "slough of despond." I want to approach this from a spiritual point of view, because the only lasting solution is from the Lord.

Depression usually follows a definite pattern. It begins with *self-protection*. You are deeply hurt in some way. Perhaps somebody failed you; or maybe some plan that you had collapsed; or perhaps you failed yourself. In some way, a hurt comes to you and this hurt threatens to rob you of your peace and enjoyment of life. The best thing to do is to face that hurt honestly and deal with it: pray about it, commit it to the Lord, and apply the medicine of God's Word. But sometimes we hurt so much that we just don't seem to have the strength to deal with it; and this is where self-protection comes in. Because you have been hurt, you pull into yourself and retreat from the realities of life. You feel safe with yourself; you don't feel safe with others.

In one sense, depression is to your heart what a callous is to your hand: it is a form of emergency protection. It helps to make that hurt area insensitive. This explains why most depressed people have no interest in life around them—their family and friends, their jobs, even their usual enjoyments. They isolate themselves because this helps to protect them from being hurt again. This brings us to the second step: self-protection leads to *self-pity*. We feel sorry for ourselves, so we pull into ourselves and retreat from life. We get all wrapped up in our own problems and pains and forget that other people have problems and pains, too.

This leads to the third step, which is *self-punishment*. You *protect* yourself by withdrawing; then you *pity* yourself because you feel so isolated; and then you start *punishing* yourself for whatever you think you have done. You become judge and jury and condemn yourself to a life of self-inflicted pain to atone for whatever wrongs you imagine you have done. It is here that Satan enters the picture, because he is the accuser of the brethren. He likes to remind you of your sins, your mistakes, your failures, even your embarrassing moments. Each of these reminders only makes the wounds in our heart hurt that much more, and then you withdraw even deeper and isolate yourself from reality.

No wonder some people try to take the next step—*self-destruction*. Satan is the destroyer, and he knows how to get a beachhead in your life just where you are the weakest. But there is an answer to this kind of depression. There is no need for you to protect yourself and pity yourself and then punish yourself. Jesus Christ can come to you and meet the need and help you to defeat depression.

When you realize that depression has attacked you, immediately surrender yourself to Jesus Christ and tell Him all about the hurt down inside. This is what the psalmist did in Psalms 42 and 43. He told the Lord how much he hurt, how disappointed he was in the way things were going. He honestly unburdened his feelings and his complaints. Instead of nursing his hurts, he gave his heart to the great physician.

The second step is to get your eyes on the Lord and off of yourself. Self-pity is one of the most dangerous attitudes you and I can ever cultivate. It poisons our system so that nothing looks right; everything people say and do gets out of proportion. Ask the Lord to give you the strength to fight self-pity! In Psalms 42 and 43 the psalmist writes: "My soul thirsteth for God, for the living God. . . . Hope thou in God, for I shall yet praise him for the help of his countenance. Yet the Lord will command his lovingkindness in the daytime, and in the night his song shall be with me. O send out thy light and thy truth: Let them lead me. . . ." In spite of his disappointment, the psalmist looks to God and sees what God can do for him. For you and me, this means looking into the promises of the Word. "O send out thy light and thy truth."

The third step is to remember that Jesus Christ died for all your sins and failures, and you need not punish yourself. When you confess your sins and failures to the Lord, He forgives and forgets. You may not *feel* that He does, but He does just the same, because this is the promise of His Word. God no longer deals with you on the basis of *law;* he deals with you on the basis of *grace.* "There is therefore now no condemnation to them that are in Christ Jesus. . . . Their sins and their iniquities will I remember no more." Why should you punish yourself when Jesus Christ bore all the punishment for you? Your Father loves you; He forgives you; He will see you through.

8

Escape or Fulfillment?

When Jesus was arrested in the Garden of Gethsemane, Peter tried to defend him with a sword. Jesus rebuked Peter and said, "Don't you know that I could ask my Father and he would give me more than twelve legions of angels? But how then should the Scriptures be fulfilled?" In this statement, Jesus is telling us that there are two ways to face the crises of life—escape or fulfillment. Which of these approaches do you follow?

There is no question that all of the armies of heaven would have been glad to hasten to Gethsemane and deliver the Son of God from the hands of sinful men. All Jesus had to do was say the word. If Peter had been in charge, he would have summoned the highest archangel and destroyed Jerusalem! But Jesus did not take that approach. He could have escaped, but it was not the will of God. Instead of facing his crisis with a philosophy of escape, Jesus faced it with a attitude of fulfillment.

We can't prevent the crisis hours of life. And the older we get, the more serious life becomes. For one thing, we realize that our decisons affect many other people. And we also realize that time is running out—we can't afford to make too many blunders. So, crisis hours do come to us; but how do we meet them? What attitude do we take when the foundations are shaking and the walls are falling down around us?

Many people take the same attitude that Peter took in the garden—the attitude of escape. Peter drew out his sword and tried to defend Jesus. It was a noble gesture, but Peter was wrong in his thinking. To begin with, Jesus doesn't need swords for defense. He could have called legions of angels had He wanted to defend Himself. But the big mistake Peter was making was this: he was preventing Jesus from fulfilling the very purpose for which He came to earth! Peter's action was zeal without knowledge. He was defending when he should have been submitting.

Before we criticize Peter too much, let's look at our own lives. How many times have we tried to escape when we should have surrendered to the will of God? Don't all of us have scars from battles that should never have been fought? I'm sure we do. Trying to escape the crisis is the natural thing to do, but this doesn't make it right. After all, as Christians we live on a much higher plane—we live by faith, not by sight.

Every life has its Gethsemane experiences. There are those hours when the forces of evil seem to swoop down upon us and capture us. All our plans fall apart. The burdens become almost unbearable. We wonder what can happen next. In those crisis hours of life just keep in mind what Jesus did— He surrendered and permitted His Father in heaven to work out His plan. Jesus did not choose escape; He chose fulfillment.

At this point you may be saying, "All of what you have said is true. But the life of Jesus is different from our lives. He came to accomplish a definite purpose, so it was natural for Him to surrender to the Father's will. Does this apply to us?" Yes, this principle of fulfillment does apply to you and me. God has a definite plan for our lives. Paul puts it this way in Ephesians 2:10: "For we are his workmanship, created in Christ Jesus unto good works, which God hath before ordained that we should walk in them." If you are yielded to Christ, your life is not a series of accidents; it is a series of appointments.

That God has a plan for you is vitally important. If God doesn't have a plan, then life has no meaning. Suffering is in vain; sacrifice is meaningless. If there is no design for our lives, then there is nothing to fulfill and the logical thing to do is escape. But there is a heavenly design. The will of God for you is the expression of His love for you. This explains that wonderful promise, Romans 8:28: "And we know that all things work together for good to them that love God, to them who are the called according to his purpose."

Not escape, but fulfillment—this is the lesson Jesus teaches us in the Garden of Gethsemane. He could have summoned the armies of heaven to deliver Him, but instead He surrendered that God's purposes might be fulfilled. And He knew when He surrendered that it would mean shame, suffering, and death. By yielding to the hands of sinful men He was actually asking for suffering! But it was the will of God, and that was all that mattered. And what was the result? Resurrection and glory! The cross was not the end; the empty tomb was the end. He fulfilled the will of God and entered into glory!

We must never mistake the process for the result. When you don't run away, but remain to face the crisis in the will of God, there is suffering; but this is only the process. God isn't going to stop with the process; He wants to produce the final result. Suffering leads to glory; shame leads to honor; weakness leads to power. This is God's way of doing things. Men will do their worst, but God will give His best. Jesus yielded into the hands of wicked men that He might fulfill the purposes of God—and those purposes were fulfilled. He paid the price for our salvation, and now any sinner can turn to God, through faith in Christ, and be saved from sin.

I don't know what crisis you may be facing just now, but I do know this: you will be tempted to escape. We've all done it. We've prayed and asked God to send His angels to deliver us. If escape is your approach to life, then you are going to miss out on all the blessings God has for you. For one thing, people who practice escape never really mature. You can't grow in faith and patience while running away. And these people never really glorify Christ. Hiding your light under an escape hatch is no way to glorify the Lord.

Escape seems to be the easy way at the time, but ultimately it becomes the hard way. I had a friend who kept putting off going to the doctor because he was afraid he would have to have surgery. When he finally did have surgery, it was too late. The crisis experiences of life are sometimes like surgery—they hurt us, but they don't harm us. The process may be painful, but the result is joyful.

You and I have yielded our lives to Jesus Christ; He is our Savior and Lord. He has promised never to leave us or to forsake us. He does not promise to deliver us out of every crisis, but He does promise to bring us through. He wants us to practice fulfillment, not escape; and He has set the example for us. In Him we see that the will of God is the best thing, the only thing. Instead of running away, run into the arms of your loving heavenly Father and let Him fulfill His wonderful purposes in your life today.

9

Living Through Disappointments

Each of us must learn how to handle the disappointments of life. All of us know what it means to have our dreams shattered and our plans changed. Sometimes disappointment so crushes a person that he is emotionally handicapped for life. And yet there are people who rise above the broken dreams and live in victory. In this meditation, I want to introduce you to a man who faced life-long disappointment and yet triumphed over it all.

If ever a man experienced disappointments and personal tragedy, it was Jeremiah. He was called to serve God at a difficult time in history. And he was given a difficult message to proclaim, for God told him to warn the nation that judgment was coming and they had better repent. Jeremiah served the Lord faithfully for over forty years. He never compromised in his message or his loyalty. His family turned against him, and ultimately the entire nation turned against him. He lived to see his beloved nation overrun by the enemy, and his beloved city and temple completely destroyed.

If ever a man had a broken heart, it was Jeremiah. His book of prophecies bears witness to his burden, and the Book of Lamentations, which he also wrote, has tear stains on almost every verse. Imagine serving God faithfully for a life time and, in the end, seeing everything fall apart! Jeremiah could have died a bitter and broken man, but he did not. In the strength of the Lord he was able to face his disappointments and accept them.

I could point you to many statements in Jeremiah's prophecy that indicate his courage and faith, but just one of them will meet the need in this message. It is found in Jeremiah 10:19: "Woe is me for my hurt! my wound is grievous: but I said, Truly this is a grief, and I must bear it." That statement is, to me, one of the greatest declarations of faith and faithfulness found anywhere in the Bible. Let's learn from the prophet Jeremiah how to face and conquer the disappointments of life.

The first truth he teaches us is this: *expect disappointments*. Life is not always going to be sunny and clear; there will be days—and perhaps weeks—when it will be stormy and dark. Some people have the idea that faithful Christians escape disappointments, but this is not true. God does not guarantee that we will never have a broken heart. God does not promise to take away our tears this side of heaven. As you read your Bible, and as you read Christian biography, you discover that the faithful saints of God have their share of disappointments.

Don't you think godly Abraham was disappointed in the behavior of his nephew Lot? Wasn't Joseph burdened at the selfish treatment he received from his brothers? The sins of the people of Israel broke the heart of Moses time after time, so much so that he even wanted to die! King David had great plans for his family, yet some of his sons were so sinful they almost wrecked the nation. As you read the letters of Paul, you learn that he too knew what it was to suffer disappointment and to have his own helpers in the ministry fail him and the Lord. The Lord never promised us an easy life, so expect disappointments.

Jeremiah did not try to fool himself into thinking everything was fine. "Woe is me for my hurt," he wrote. "My wound is grievous." He admitted that his heart was broken. He openly confessed that he had been wounded by those who should have caused him joy. Expect disappointment; it is one of the hard facts of life.

The prophet Jeremiah teaches us a second truth: *our disappointments are in the hands of God.* I am sure there were many times when the prophet thought he had been forsaken by God. Why wasn't God answering his prayers? Why wasn't the Word he was preaching bearing fruit and changing the nation? Was it really worth it all staying there and ministering to such hardhearted people?

God knew what was happening, and God was ruling and overruling in Jeremiah's life. God permitted His servant to suffer. God protected him when the king wanted to kill him, and God provided for him so he did not go hungry. God even knew how Jeremiah would die, and He did not prevent it. God was there whether or not Jeremiah saw Him or felt His presence.

The first lie that the enemy whispers to us when disappointment comes is that God has failed. Perhaps you have received a doctor's report, and the report is not what you expected. You prayed, you read your Bible and claimed God's promises, and still the disappointment came. Does this mean that God has failed? No, it does not. Does it mean that we have failed God? Not necessarily. Jeremiah was faithful to serve God even to the point of death, and yet he did not live to see his dreams for his people fulfilled.

Dr. A. T. Pierson used to say, "Disappointments are His appointments." It takes faith to believe that and rest upon it, but it is true God is still on the throne, and He is going to accomplish His wonderful purposes in our lives, if we will let Him. If we fight circumstances and become bitter, then God cannot accomplish in us and through us all that He has in mind. If we yield and trust Him to do what is best, then all things will work together for good.

Listen to Jeremiah's declaration of faith as he faces the painful disappointments of life: "Woe is me for my hurt! my wound is grievous: But I said, Truly this is a grief, and I must bear it.'' He did not blame God or other people; he did not try to "pass the buck"; he did not fight circumstances and try to change God's mind. He accepted by faith the burden of his grief, and he trusted God to work out His perfect will. There is a basic law in this universe that says, "Fight the will of God and it will break you; accept the will of God and it will make you.'' Which will you do?

We have learned two helpful truths about the disappointments of life: first, expect them; second, believe that God is working out a perfect plan. The third truth is this: *yield to God's will and let Him heal your broken heart and fulfill His desires*. Jeremiah did not fight God, although there were times when he questioned God's will. He did not try to get his own way. Instead Jeremiah yielded to the will of God and let God work out His perfect plan.

What was the result? The nation was taken captive and carried to Babylon. And Jeremiah was kidnapped and taken to Egypt by some fanatics, and there, according to tradition, he was stoned to death for preaching the truth. The story does not have a happy ending, but in the will of God, every ending is a happy one. God does not judge a man's life by what the newspapers say. He judges righteously on the basis of what is eternal.

What did God accomplish in this tragic history? For one thing, God made a man who was very much like the Lord Jesus Christ. When Jesus was here on earth, He asked His disciples what people were saying about Him; and one of the answers was, "You are the prophet Jeremiah." What a tremendous compliment, to be compared to the Lord Jesus Christ! When you read Jeremiah's life, you can find many parallels between him and the Savior—and the thing that made him that way was his suffering. The very disappointments of life were the tools that carved Jeremiah and polished him and made him like Jesus Christ.

Isn't that what disappointments are all about? God is working all things together for good, and part of that good (according to Romans 8:29) is that we might be conformed to the image of His Son—made more like the Lord Jesus Christ. The four men in the Old Testament who best picture Jesus Christ are men who suffered—Joseph, Moses, David, and Jeremiah. So, if you and I suffer, it is because God wants to polish us and make us like His own Son.

God builds character in the disappointments of life and He also gives a witness. In the midst of his disappointments, Jeremiah bore witness to the Lord and gave His message to the people. By his preaching and his living, Jeremiah pointed others to God. Disappointments are not only opportunities for maturity, but they are also opportunities for ministry. We today have the writings of Jeremiah for our own learning and living because the prophet was faithful to God. When you accept disappointments, trust God, and yield to Him, you leave something behind to help others in the battles of life.

"Truly this is a grief, and I must bear it!" wrote Jeremiah. He did not complain about it—he accepted his disappointments and let God use them for his good and for the glory of God.

10

Under His Wings

In 1892, after a year of intensive work in Great Britain, D. L. Moody sailed for home, eager to get back to his family and his work. The ship left Southampton amid many farewells. About three days out into the ocean, the ship ground to a halt with a broken shaft; and before long, it began to take water. Needless to say, the crew and passengers were desperate, because nobody was sure whether the vessel would sink or not, and nobody knew of any rescue ships in the area. After two days of anxiety, Moody asked for permission to hold a meeting, and to his surprise, nearly every passenger attended. He opened his Bible to Psalm 91 and, holding to a pillar to steady himself, he read: "He that dwelleth in the secret place of the Most High shall abide under the shadow of the Almighty."

Moody wrote later, "It was the darkest hour of my life . . . relief came in prayer. God heard my cry, and enabled me to say, from the depth of my soul, 'Thy will be done.' I went to bed and fell asleep almost immediately. . . ." Well, God answered prayer and saved the ship and sent another vessel to tow it to port. Psalm 91 became a vibrant new Scripture to D. L. Moody, and he discovered, as you and I must also discover, that the safest place in the world is in the shadow of the Almighty, "under His wings."

"He that dwelleth in the secret place of the Most High

shall abide under the shadow of the Almighty . . . . He shall cover thee with his feathers, and under his wings shalt thou trust . . . ." So promises the Lord in Psalm 91:1, 4. What does God mean by "under His wings"? Of course, we know that this is symbolical language, because God does not have wings. Some think that this has reference to the way the mother hen shelters and protects her brood. You will remember that Jesus used a similar comparison when He said, "How oft would I have gathered you, as a hen gathers her chickens under her wings, and you would not."

My own conviction is that Psalm 91 is talking about another kind of wings. Where is that secret place of the Most High? To every Old Testament Jew, there was only one secret place—the holy of holies in the tabernacle. You will recall that the tabernacle was divided into three parts: an outer court where the sacrifices were offered; a holy place where the priests burned the incense; and then the holy of holies where the ark of the covenant was kept. And you will remember that over the ark of the covenant, on the mercy seat, were two cherubim, and their wings overshadowed the ark. This, I believe, is what the psalmist was referring to: the "secret place," is the holy of holies, and "the shadow of the Almighty" is under the wings of the cherubim at the mercy seat.

In Old Testament days, no one was permitted to enter that holy of holies, except the high priest; and he could do it only once a year. If anyone tried to force his way in, he was killed. But today, all of God's children, saved by faith in Jesus Christ, can enter the holy of holies, because Jesus Christ has opened the way for us. When Jesus died on the cross, the veil in the temple was torn in two and the way was opened into the very presence of God. You and I are privileged to dwell in the holy of holies—to live under the shadow of His wings. We don't simply make occasional visits into God's presence; we live there because of Jesus Christ!

Would you believe it if I told you that the safest place in

the world is under a shadow? It is—provided that the shadow is the shadow of the Almighty! I would rather be overshadowed by Almighty God than protected by the mightiest army in the world.

As you read Psalm 91, you discover that God makes some marvelous promises to those who will live under His wings, in the holy of holies. For one thing, He promises divine protection. This doesn't mean that we Christians never experience accidents or sickness, because you and I know that we do. God does not promise to protect us *from* trials, but to protect us *in* trials. The dangers of life may *hurt* us but they can never *harm* us. We can claim His promise that these things are working for us and not against us.

Listen to one of these promises: "He shall give His angels charge over thee, to keep thee in all thy ways. They shall bear thee up in their hands lest thou dash thy foot against a stone." A modern scientific world laughs at the idea of angels, but not the child of God. Jesus taught that the angels of God watch over God's children. The angels don't run ahead of us and pick up the stones, because sometimes we need these stones in the path to teach us to depend more on the Lord. What the angels do is help us use the stones for stepping stones, not stumbling blocks. I firmly believe that when we get to heaven, we will discover how many times God's angels have watched over us and saved our lives. This is not an encouragement to be careless or to tempt God, but it is an encouragement to worry less.

A man is immortal in the will of God, until his work is done. Out of the will of God there is danger, but in the will of God there is a divine protection that gives a man peace in his heart, no matter how trying life may be. "Under His wings," abiding in Christ—this is where we are safest during the storms of life.

We do not, however, run into the holy of holies to hide from life. I'm afraid too many people misinterpret the Scriptures and the hymns that talk about hiding in God and finding Him a refuge in the storm. We go in for strength and help, and then go back to life to do His will. God's divine protection is not simply a luxury we enjoy; it is a necessity that we want to share with others. God's protection is preparation for God's service. We go *in* that we might go *out*. We worship that we might work; we rest that we might serve.

Are you living in the shadow of the Lord, under His wings? Have you trusted Christ as your Savior? Do you spend time daily in worship and prayer? I trust that you do, because the safest life and the most satisfying life is under His wings.

The person who lives under His wings not only enjoys the safest life possible, but also the most satisfying life possible. Psalm 91 closes with this promise. "With long life will I satisfy him, and show him my salvation." This doesn't mean that all Christians will live to be a hundred; the facts prove otherwise. Some of the choicest Christians died before age thirty. A long life refers to *quality,* not just *quantity:* it means a full and satisfying life. You can live for eighty years and only exist if you leave Christ out. On the other hand, if you yield to Christ, you can pour into forty years three or four lifetimes of service and enjoyment. There is a heart satisfaction that comes only to those who live under His wings, in the place of surrender and fellowship.

The place of satisfaction is the secret place of the Most High. When you yield to Jesus Christ and link your life with Him, then you find the kind of satisfaction that is worth living for and worth dying for—not the shallow masquerades of this world, but the deep abiding peace and joy that can come only from Jesus Christ.

Turn your back on sin and the cheap trinkets that this world offers, and let me invite you to enter the secret place of the Most High. Surrender to Christ; trust Him as your Savior; answer His gracious invitation. When you do this, you will enter into a new kind of life—a life under the shadow of God—a life in the secret place of safety and satisfaction.

11

Honey out of the Rock

One of God's promises to His children recorded in Psalm 81:16, is that He will satisfy us with "honey out of the rock." Of course, you and I know that honey is perhaps the sweetest thing that nature can produce; and a rock is one of the hardest things in nature. So, here we have sweetness coming out of hardness—"honey out of the rock." This is one of God's promises, and you should claim it for yourself.

God is not speaking in literal terms in Psalm 81:16; you and I get honey either from the honeycomb or from a jar. The Lord is saying something much deeper: "You are going to have hard places in life; you are going to run up against the rocks. But don't be discouraged: I'm going to give you honey out of the rock. You're going to experience sweetness out of the hard experiences of life."

I used to wonder why God didn't *remove* the rocks from the path of life. Certainly none of us enjoys going through the hard places, and if God really loved us, He would go ahead of us and remove the rocks. Well, I've grown some and I've come to realize that God knows what He is doing. You and I don't appreciate the rocks, but we need them just the same. I'm sure you have learned, as I have, that some of the sweetest experiences of life have come because of the rocks.

This was certainly true of people in Bible days. I think of

young Joseph who seemed to have nothing but rocks for thirteen years. First he was hated by his own brothers. Then he was sold into Egypt as a slave. Then, because he would not stoop to commit sin, he was thrown into prison and apparently forgotten. It was just one rocky experience after another, and seemingly for no purpose! But when it was over—when God had fulfilled His purposes—Joseph discovered honey out of the rock. These hard experiences prepared him to become God's servant and the second ruler over Egypt.

David had similar experiences. He was anointed king of Israel, yet he was hunted like a common criminal. King Saul hated him and tried to kill him. David had to flee his home and live in caves. If ever a man went through rocky experiences, David did. I suppose more than once David had his doubts and heard the enemy say, "It's not worth it to serve the Lord. Why don't you give up? God promised you a kingdom, and all you've had so far are rocks and caves." David didn't give up, and one day God gave him honey out of the rock. In fact, many of the psalms that encourage our hearts today were born out of David's difficult experiences of life.

One of the tests of maturity is how a person gets his enjoyment in life. Some get their pleasures by doing what is wrong, and, of course, this is the lowest possible way to live. Others get their pleasure by avoiding responsibilities and difficulties and being sheltered and protected. That approach to life can never make a person strong and mature. The mature Christian doesn't deliberately look for difficulties, but neither does he run away from them. Rather he accepts them in the will of God and asks the Lord to give him "honey out of the rock."

I've noticed that many of the psalms have three divisions: tears, trust, and triumph. The psalm begins with tears and trouble, and the psalmist cries out to God. Then he gets his eyes off himself and his difficulties and looks to God in faith. When he does a wonderful thing happens: his trials are replaced by triumph, and his sighing becomes singing. He has discovered honey out of the rock.

This is what James is trying to teach us in the very first verses of his letter, when he writes: "My brethren, count it all joy when you encounter various kinds of testings; knowing this, that the trial of your faith worketh patience. . . ." Trials are not working against us; they are working *for* us! James is saying, "Don't run around the rocks, or stand there and expect God to remove them. Instead, look for the honey that is sure to come from the rocks!" Paul says the same thing when he writes, "And we know that all things work together for good to them that love God, to them that are the called according to his purpose" (Rom. 8:28). No matter how many rocks we may encounter as we go through life, we can always find "honey in the rocks" if we will turn everything over to the Lord.

Right now you may be going through a hard place. You've been faithfully doing your job, yet you are right up against a rock, and the rock won't move. Ask God to give you the honey out of the rock. There is always sweetness out of hardness when you let the Lord have His way.

Everybody has to have a system for handling the hard places of life. Some people try to ignore them and pretend that they don't exist, and, of course, this only makes the hard places harder. Other people just give up and expect their friends to see them through. It is wonderful to have friends, and we are supposed to share each other's burdens, but we can't expect them to do for us what we won't do for ourselves.

Have you ever considered the difficulties that Jesus faced when He lived here on earth. He was born into a poor home and never really owned much that He could call His own. He was born into a despised and rejected race, a minority group, which at that time, was under the iron heel of a foreign power. Whenever Jesus tried to do good, somebody tried to turn it into evil. If He stopped to forgive a sinner, He was called "the friend of publicans and sinners." If He ate a meal with a friend, He was called a "glutton and a drunkard." He spoke the truth and was called a liar. He revealed the power of God, and the religious leaders said He was in league with the devil. No matter where He turned or what He did, He faced hard situations.

But Jesus never ran away from the hard places of life. He knew He was doing the Father's will, so He accepted the rocks and the honey that was in them. He said to His disciples one day when they offered Him food, "My food is to do the will of him that sent me and to finish his work." He found the honey in the rock, and that honey satisfied Him.

Yes, Jesus faced the rocks of life, and finally men took Him outside the city and crucified Him on a rock, a hill called Calvary, a place that looked like a skull. And then His friends took His dead body and placed it in a rock—Joseph's new tomb—it lay for three days. But then He arose from the dead! From the hill of Calvary and from the tomb flows the sweet honey of salvation—honey out of the rock!

Have you trusted Christ as your Savior? God says, "O taste and see that the Lord is good!" Once you know Christ as your Savior and Lord, then you can face the hard places of life with confidence and courage, because God will give you "honey out of the rock."

12

How to Keep Going

He knew that wherever he went there would be trouble and pain and persecution. Some of his friends warned him to protect himself and escape. But the great apostle Paul was not the kind of person that ran away from difficulty or challenge. This is why, in Acts 20:24, he said to his friends, "But none of these things move me, neither count I my life dear unto myself, so that I might finish my course with joy, and the ministry, which I have received of the Lord Jesus, to testify the Gospel of the grace of God."

Three phrases stand out boldly in this testimony: my life, my course, my ministry. Let's look at them individually and try to discover some of the secrets of Paul's courage and devotion.

The first phrase is *"my life."* Paul said, "Neither count I my life dear unto myself . . . ." He learned this truth from the Lord Jesus Christ. You will remember that Jesus told His disciples, "He that saveth his life shall lose it, but he that loseth his life for my sake and the Gospel's, the same shall save it." He also said, "If any man will come after me, let him deny himself, and take up his cross, and follow me."

Your life is a gift from God. "In him we live, and move, and have our being." Even before you were born, God knew you and had a purpose for your life. Your talents and abilities, your interests, your strengths, and even your weaknesses, are all a part of a divine plan. God gave you natural life, but He also gave you spiritual life through faith in Jesus Christ. God made you and God saved you. The life you have, physically and spiritually, is the gift of God.

Paul did not keep this gift for himself. He gave it back to God for Him to use for the glory of Jesus Christ. He said, "Neither count I my life dear unto myself. . . ." There is a principle in the spiritual life that says: whatever you keep, you lose; whatever you give, you possess forever. If you count your life dear to yourself, and protect your own interests, and pamper yourself, then you will never really live. But if you yield yourself to the Lord and let Him control your life, you will enjoy abundant life.

Selfish people are always unhappy people. They are so busy trying to get more that they fail to enjoy what they already have. When you go through life asking, "What am I going to get?" Instead of "What can I give?" you lose out on all the exciting blessings God has for those who turn their lives over to Him. Paul did not make his own life the dearest thing. It was the will of God that was uppermost in Paul's life. He wrote to the Galatian Christians, "Not I, but Christ liveth in me. . . ." His life was not a treasure for him to *guard;* it was a treasure for him to *invest* by yielding to Jesus Christ. You and I have but one life to live. When life is ended, there will be no more opportunity to make that life count for Christ.

Paul uses a second phrase in Acts 20:24: *"my course."* He says, "Neither count I my life dear unto myself, that I might finish my course with joy. . . ." That word *course* suggests a race with Paul as one of the runners. Paul often used athletic illustrations in his letters, and this is one of them. No doubt he had often seen the athletic games in various Greek cities, and they suggested to him truths about the Christian life.

No one could compete in the Greek games unless he were a citizen. Well, no one can run in the Christian race unless he is a child of God, a citizen of heaven. When you give your heart to Jesus Christ, He saves you and takes you off that broad road that leads to destruction. He puts you on the narrow road that leads to heaven, and He assigns a track for you on the course. In Philippians 3 and Hebrews 12, God compares the Christian life to a race, and He assigns each Christian runner his own special lane. The important thing is that we obey the rules, keep running for the prize, and stay in the correct lane. If we do, then God will reward us at the end of the course. If we fail to run as we should, we will lose our reward.

What keeps us from running the race as we should? Sometimes we get out of training. Just as an athlete must stay in training, so the Christian must obey the Lord and be careful about his spiritual disciplines. Hebrews 12:1 warns us about excessive weight and the sin that causes us to stumble. There are some things that we Christians give up, not because they are sinful in themselves, but because they keep us from running a good race. Athletes need proper diet, fresh air, and proper rest—and so do we as Christian athletes. We need to feed on the Word of God, breathe the pure air of heaven as we pray, and rest in the Lord and trust Him for the strength we need.

Paul's great ambition was to finish *his* course, not someone else's. As Christians running the race, we are not in competition with other believers; because *all* of us can win the race and get a reward. No, we are in competition with *ourselves*. Are we farther along the course today than we were last week? Or have we slipped back and lost ground spiritually? Please don't measure yourself by some other Christian. Measure yourself by the plan God has for your life, the prize He wants you to win.

One of the worst things a runner can do is keep looking back. Paul writes in Philippians 3, "Forgetting those things which are behind. . . ." Let's keep our eyes on the goal; let's be sure we are running in the lane God has assigned to us. Let the Lord take care of the other runners. Jesus says to us as

He did to Peter, "What is that to thee? Follow thou me."

Paul wanted to finish his course with joy, and he did. We read his words in II Timothy 4:7: "I have fought a good fight, I have finished my course, I have kept the faith." He was looking forward to seeing the Lord Jesus Christ and sharing in that crown of righteousness. The race would soon be over, and the prize of the high calling would soon be his. One day the race will be over for you and for me. Will we be able to say, "I have finished my course with joy?"

The last of the three phrases that Paul uses in Acts 20:24 is *"my ministry"*—"the ministry, which I have received of the Lord." His life was a gift from God. His course was assigned by God. While he was running that course, he wanted more than anything else to fulfill the ministry the Lord had given him.

Each of us has a ministry to fulfill. Paul wrote to young Timothy, "Make full proof of thy ministry." Literally that means, "Fulfill your ministry; accomplish in your work the things God has called you to do." Each of us has a special ministry from the Lord that no one can do for us. It is *our* ministry, assigned to us by the Lord, and we are responsible to finish it for His glory. We never should envy somebody else because of his or her ministry, because the work God has given us to do is just as important in the eyes of God.

Paul's ministry centered in sharing the gospel of the grace of God. That word *grace* is a marvelous word! It carries with it the idea of God's free gifts to people who do not deserve them. Grace is God's favor. You cannot earn it; you cannot merit it; you can only receive it by faith. Grace means that God does for you what you cannot do for yourself. Grace means that God gives to you what you could never earn or deserve if you tried for a million years. Paul was the great ambassador of the grace of God.

Whatever ministry God has called you to fulfill, be sure to magnify the grace of God. Most of the people in the world think they can earn their way to heaven, or please God by good works and religious activities. It is our privilege and responsibility to tell them the gospel—the good news—that God will give them salvation if they will only receive Christ and trust Him. Salvation by works would be bad news, because nobody could ever make it; but salvation by grace is good news—anybody can trust Jesus Christ and be saved.

My life—my course—my ministry. It would do us good to repeat those three phrases at the beginning of each day, for they help us take inventory of our spiritual experience. Am I holding my life dear to myself, or do I yield my life to Christ? Am I running on the course God has assigned to me? Am I fulfilling the ministry that He has given me? No matter what problems you may be facing just now, turn yourself over to Jesus Christ. Yield Him your life and let Him work out His perfect will in you—in your life, your course, and your ministry.

13

Through
the Furnace of Pain

Nearly two hundred years ago, Thomas Jefferson wrote a letter to his friend Mrs. Cosway, and in it he said, "The art of life is the avoiding of pain." Thomas Jefferson was a great man and a brilliant thinker, but I disagree. When we first hear that statement, it appears to be true. None of us deliberately looks for pain as we go about our daily activities. When it comes time for our six-month's dental check-up or our annual visit to the doctor, we really wish we didn't have to go. After all, the dentist might have to fill a cavity, or the doctor might order an operation or a diet! Generally speaking, all of us do our best to avoid pain.

But when you take a deeper look at the statement, you see that it fails to live up to the facts of history. Thomas Jefferson himself paid a price to help lead the American Revolution! Many of the patriots of that day lost their names, their homes, their fortunes, and some their lives, in order to win liberty. Our liberty was purchased by pain and death; and our liberty has been protected by pain and death. History itself shows us that human progress can only be made when somebody suffers for that which is true and right.

Even apart from history, our own personal experience teaches us the folly of this statement. The deepest pains are not physical; they are emotional and spiritual. All of us have suffered pain during our pilgrimage of life. We could have avoided the pain, but we have learned that the most important things in life usually involve suffering. If people lived to avoid pain, they would never want to grow up. But just think of what they would miss!

Take the matter of human birth. To be sure, we have modern scientific methods to protect mothers, but there is still a certain amount of pain. Jesus Himself used this as an illustration of His own suffering when He said, "A woman when she is in travail has sorrow because her hour is come; but as soon as she is delivered of the child, she remembers no more the anguish, for joy that a man is born into the world."

Think, too, of the pain and sorrow that the mother and father experience as they seek to raise that child. The old proverb says, "When they are little, children step on your feet; but when they are older, they step on your heart." Often this is true. In my ministry I have met dedicated Christian parents whose hearts have been broken because of wayward children who failed to heed their instruction and example. If everybody really lived to avoid pain, nobody would get married and raise a family; yet people do it all the time.

We must never think that pain is something sinful. Some suffering comes because of disobedience; but not all pain is the result of sin. If Adam in the Garden of Eden had tripped over a rock, he would have felt it. To be sure, the pain of sickness and physical decline is ultimately caused by sin; but even the pain of sickness can have a good result. If you and I never felt pain when something was wrong in our bodies, we would die from neglect. A pain somewhere in the body is a danger signal, and we ought to be thankful for it.

But for the Christian believer, pain has much higher ministries. I often hear people say that Christians suffer more than other people do, but I'm not so sure this can be proved. As I visit hospitals and nursing homes, I meet many unsaved people who are suffering. In fact, I believe that the dedicated Christian probably avoids a lot of the physical suffering that comes to a person who defiles and destroys his body through sin and selfishness.

What are the higher ministries of pain? Well, for one thing, pain can have a purifying power. The apostle Peter writes in I Peter 4:1, "For he that has suffered in the flesh hath ceased from sin." One of the modern translations puts it, "You must realize then that to be dead to sin inevitably means pain." I once went through intense physical suffering, and it very definitely had a purifying effect on my heart and mind. It made me see spiritual things a lot more clearly. My priorities were rearranged. Granted, pain *by itself* can never accomplish this; but when we yield to Christ and ask for His help, pain can purify us.

A secondary ministry of pain is that of fellowship with Christ. In Philippians 3:10 Paul writes about "the fellowship of his [Christ's] sufferings." Some people turn against God when they go through suffering, but this need not be so. You and I can be drawn closer to God by faith when we are going through the furnace of pain. None of us has ever experienced all that Jesus experienced on the cross. The unsaved person has no idea of the wonderful joy and peace the believer experiences in his heart even in the midst of constant pain.

A third ministry of pain is bringing glory to God. This doesn't mean that God deliberately makes us suffer just so He can receive glory. But it does mean that God can use our suffering to glorify His name. When Jesus faced the hour of His death, He said, "Father, glorify thy name." And God was glorified in the suffering and death of His Son, and God honored Christ and raised Him from the dead in great glory. I have visited Christians in hospitals and homes whose lives were glorifying God even in their suffering.

Pain purifies. Pain draws the Christian closer to Christ. Pain glorifies God. But we must also remember that pain today means glory and honor tomorrow. Paul wrote, "The sufferings of this present time are not worthy to be compared with the glory that shall be revealed in us." God doesn't always settle His accounts in this life. In fact, no Christian should expect to receive much reward in this world. Jesus said, "In the world you shall have tribulation." A man said to me one day, "I don't believe in hell or heaven. You have your hell or heaven here on earth." That man was wrong. The unsaved person had better enjoy this world all he can because it's the only heaven he will ever see! "It is appointed unto men once to die and after that the judgment."

But the Christian is looking forward to the glory of heaven. Jim Eliot, one of the martyred missionaries of Ecuador, wrote in his journal: "He is no fool to give what he cannot keep, to gain what he cannot lose." If we suffer with Christ today, it only means glory with Christ tomorrow. For the Christian, the best is yet to come.

Have you surrendered your pain to Christ and asked Him to use it for your good and His glory? I suggest that you do so by faith. God doesn't promise to remove our pain, or even to relieve our pain; but He does promise to transform it and use it for His eternal purposes.

The great apostle Paul was in pain. He had a thorn in the flesh, given to him by God to help keep him humble and useful. Paul did what any Christian would have done—he prayed for the pain to be removed. God did not answer his prayer, but He did meet his need. He gave Paul all the grace he needed to transform that weakness to strength, that suffering into glory. And God will give grace to you and me if only we will yield our all to Him.

14

After the Victory

Andrew Bonar was a saintly Presbyterian minister in Scotland who lived a long and useful life. He was a close friend of D. L. Moody and taught Mr. Moody many things about the Bible and the Christian life. Many of his sayings have been preserved for us, and one of them in particular has caught my attention: "Let us be as watchful after the victory as before the battle." This statement parallels Paul's warning in Ephesians 6: "Wherefore take unto you the whole armor of God that you may be able to withstand in the evil day, and having done all, to stand." It is possible to win the battle and then lose the victory.

We Christians do face battles. We fight against Satan and his wiles; we also fight against this world system that has turned away from God. And, we have a battle with the flesh, too; our old nature wants to lead us into disobedience. The Christian life is not a playground; it is a battleground, and we must be on our guard at all times. We never know when Satan will tempt us. Peter writes, "Be sober, be vigilant, for your adversary the devil is walking about seeking whom he may devour." But sometimes Satan doesn't come as a roaring lion; he comes as a deceiving serpent, and we must be able to detect his traps and avoid them.

Paul warns us, "Let him that thinketh he standeth take heed lest he fall." The most dangerous time—the time that requires the most vigilance—is when we have won a victory. For some reason, after a victory, we let down our guard, we get over-confident, and this gives the enemy a chance to get in and defeat us.

This is what happened to the prophet Elijah after his great victory on Mt. Carmel. You recall that the fire came down from heaven and devoured the sacrifice, thus proving that Elijah's god was the true God of Israel. Then Elijah destroyed the false prophets and priests and waited for the nation to return and repent. But the nation didn't repent, they went on just the way they did before the great contest on the mountain. Discouraged and defeated, Elijah fled for his life and went into the desert to pout; he even asked God to take his life! Yes, Elijah won the battle, but lost the victory.

Nothing opens the door to defeat like over-confidence after a great victory. When Joshua and the armies of Israel were conquering the Promised Land, they captured the walled city of Jericho without any difficulty; but the little city of Ai turned out to be a disastrous defeat. Why? Because they were over-confident. They decided that it was a little city, in contrast to the great city of Jericho, and they reasoned that if they could capture Jericho, they ought to be able to take Ai hands down. But they didn't take Ai; they were humiliated and defeated. In their over-confidence, they had forgotten to ask God's guidance, and because there was sin in the camp, their army was defeated.

Often there are difficult testings after great victories. Moses and Israel crossed the Red Sea in great victory and watched the armies of Egypt sink in the waters; but three days later the people were thirsting for water, and the water they did find was bitter. Instead of trusting the God who had redeemed them, the people began to complain. Yes, they had won the battle, but they had lost the victory.

After the Lord Jesus and His apostles had fed the five thousand with a few loaves and fishes, Jesus commanded the twelve to get in the boat and go over to the other side of the

Sea of Galilee. I'm sure the men hated to leave that crowd, because now they were very popular leaders. What a tremendous thing it was to feed that many people with so little! As they started across the sea, a storm arose and before long the men were terrified and crying out in fear. Instead of trusting Jesus to see them through, they gave up in despair. On land, they had won the battle; but on sea, they lost the victory.

It is significant that immediately after Jesus was baptized and God spoke from heaven and the Holy Spirit came down like a dove, then Jesus was led by the Spirit into the lonely wilderness to be tempted by the devil. It is one thing to trust God when you see the Spirit like a dove, but it is quite something else to trust God when you are hungry and alone and being assailed by temptation. Yet Jesus did not lose the victory; He defeated Satan once and for all. One of our Lord's most difficult times came immediately after an experience of joy and victory and blessing.

I'm sure that your experience, as well as mine, proves that great testings usually follow great victories. For this reason it is important that we follow Andrew Bonar's advice, "Let us be as watchful after the victory as before the battle." But let's try to understand why God permits these testings to follow our triumphs.

To begin with, I think the Lord knows that *our lives need balance.* Just as creation is balanced with day and night, winter and summer, so our lives are balanced with various kinds of experiences. It is a great encouragement to know that God is in control of the circumstances of life as we walk in obedience to Him. If there is a victory, He is the One who gave it. If there is a testing after victory, He is the One who permitted it. We never have to be afraid of the seeming contradictory experiences of life because our times are in His hands.

But there is another reason why testings often follow triumphs: *the battles help us discover how much we really learned from the blessings.* Elijah saw God send fire from heaven, yet Elijah ran for his life when Queen Jezebel threatened to kill him. Isn't the God who answers by fire able to protect His own servant? Of course He is! Or, take the apostles—they saw Jesus multiply a few loaves and fishes and realized what power He possessed, but somehow they couldn't trust Him to take care of them during the storm!

The battle shows us what God can do; but the keeping of the victory shows what you and I are really made of. We get to know God better during the battle, but we get to know ourselves better during the victory. Elijah discovered God's power on Mt. Carmel, and his own weakness on Mt. Horeb. The disciples discovered Christ's power on land, but their own unbelief on the sea. The miracle of feeding the five thousand was the lesson for the day; but the storm was the examination after the lesson. Too often we don't learn the lesson until after we have failed the examination.

This leads us to a basic truth that I hope will help all of us in the days to come: *never doubt during the victory what God has taught you during the battle.* Beware of over-confidence. When you start feeling over-confident, turn to the Lord and plead for His grace and mercy; because over-confidence opens the door for the enemy to rob us of the victory. This is why Jesus said, "Watch and pray." Keep your eyes open! Put no confidence in the flesh, no matter how good you may feel. Most of our losses don't take place during the battle; they take place after the victory.

15

Blueprint for Guidance

Does God still guide His people today? Certainly He guided Abraham and Moses and the apostle Paul. But will He guide us? Can we come to the Lord and ask Him to give us the direction we need in the decisions of life? God's Word says we can: "Trust in the Lord with all thine heart, and lean not unto thine own understanding. In all thy ways acknowledge him, and he shall direct thy paths!" (Prov. 3:5, 6).

The longer we live, the more we realize our great need for the guidance of God. The prophet Jeremiah puts it very clearly when he writes, "O Lord, I know that the way of man is not in himself: it is not in man that walketh to direct his steps." If you and I are left to ourselves, we make mistakes and get lost; but if we let the Lord direct us, then the path opens up. The first step in getting the guidance of God for our lives is admitting that we need it. If we feel self-sufficient, then God cannot guide us. But if we recognize our own limitations and admit them to God, then He can lead us. It takes faith to get guidance. This is true even in the everyday activities of life. Most of us have had the experience of being in a strange place, trying to find an address. Usually we stop someone on the street, or we try to find a policeman, and we ask for information. We have faith that the stranger we ask is going to lead us to the right place. If we are making decisions about some specific problem in life, we usually go to an expert—a doctor, lawyer, or banker—and we trust that expert to give us the right counsel.

This is why Proverbs 3:5, 6 begins with faith—"Trust in the Lord with all thine heart. . . ." God wants us to trust Him with our lives, and He promises never to lead us astray. "He leadeth me in the paths of righteousness for His name's sake" is the way David explains it in Psalm 23. Certainly we can trust the Lord, because He is all-knowing, and He loves us and will never give us the wrong guidance. He has a perfect plan for our lives, and He wants us to follow His plan.

Of course, you cannot trust someone who is a stranger to you. You must know Jesus Christ as your own Savior and Lord if you want Him to direct you. When you surrender to Christ, then God becomes your Father, and Christ becomes your Shepherd, and the Holy Spirit becomes your Teacher; and together they direct you into the will of God. The unbeliever is walking in the darkness, but the child of God is walking in the light. "The path of the just is as the shining light that shineth more and more unto the perfect day."

But Proverbs 3:5 indicates that our faith in the Lord must not be half-hearted, but whole-hearted: "Trust in the Lord with all thine heart. . . ." James reminds us that "a double-minded man is unstable in all his ways." And Jesus warns us that no man can serve two masters. If there are any areas of disobedience or rebellion in our hearts, God will not guide us. But if we are yielded wholly to Him, then He has promised to direct our steps. But there is a warning attached: "lean not unto thine own understanding."

When God warns us not to "lean" on our own understanding, He is not suggesting that we stop using our brains. Many people have the strange idea that God's guidance is given to us by means of feelings or voices or magical circumstances; but such is not the case. God communicates His truth to us in our minds, through the Word of God. Often the Bible talks about loving God with the mind or having the mind renewed by the Holy Spirit. When God guides us, He does not bypass the mind; He uses it.

The warning here is that we not *depend* on our own natural reasonings. Isaiah the prophet reminds us that God's thoughts are not our thoughts, neither are His ways our ways. It is foolish to think that the natural mind can compete with the mind of God! To lean on your own understanding means to depend on your own experience, your own thinking, and not to submit it to the will of God. Certainly God wants me to think and weigh things as I consider the decisions of life, but He does not want me to depend wholly upon my own reasoning.

Let's take some Bible examples of this principle. When young David showed up at the army camp and discovered Goliath frightening the soldiers, he immediately offered to challenge the giant. David had seen God help him kill the lion and the bear, and he knew God could conquer the giant. But David's brothers laughed at him, and King Saul tried to outfit him in a suit of armor that didn't even fit. These men were leaning on their own understanding; David was following the guidance of God.

When the soldiers arrested Jesus in the Garden of Gethsemane, Peter tried to defend Him with his sword. That was the reasonable thing to do, but it was wrong in the eyes of God. Jesus rebuked Peter and then healed the damage he had done. There are times when the reasonable thing is not necessarily the Scriptural thing. It seemed unreasonable for Noah to build a boat on dry land and for Joshua to march around Jericho for a week, but these things were in the will of God.

As we read our Bibles and pray, we will discover the Spirit of God renewing our minds, and enabling us to think God's thoughts. God communicates with us in our minds through His Word. We should lean on His divine revelation, not on our natural intelligence. God puts no premium on ignorance, but neither does He depend on our IQ. There are two conditions we must meet if God is going to guide us: trust and obey. "Trust in the Lord with all thine heart, and lean not unto thine own understanding." That's trust. And Proverbs 3:6 says, "In all thy ways acknowledge him, and he shall direct thy paths." That's obedience. True faith always leads to obeying God's will. Noah believed God and proved it by obeying God and building an ark. Abraham believed God and proved it by leaving his native country and going to an unknown land.

Notice the repetition of the little word *all* in Proverbs 3:5-6—"all thine heart. . . . all thy ways. . . ." If we obey God in the things He has revealed to us, then we can be sure of His direction in the things He has not yet revealed to us. If we will do the next thing He tells us to do, then He will reveal more of His will in the days to come. God does not reveal His will all at once; He reveals it a step at a time, a day at a time. Jesus said in John 7:17, "If any man will do his will, he shall know of the doctrine. . . ." Phillips Brooks used to say that obedience is the organ of spiritual knowledge. We don't understand God's will and then obey it; we obey God's will and then He gives us the understanding.

The thing that turns off God's leading in our lives is disobedience, sin. "If I regard iniquity in my heart, the Lord will not hear me." As you seek the direction of God for your life, you certainly want to read the Bible and pray, because God uses the Word and prayer to speak to us. But it is equally as important that we obey God and acknowledge Him in all that we do. If we do something that cannot be used to acknowledge and honor God, then we are out of His will.

God has a blueprint for our lives, and in His love He wants to fulfill this plan, but He needs our cooperation. The formula in Proverbs 3:5-6 is really quite simple—trust and obey. "Trust in the Lord with all thine heart, and lean not unto thine own understanding; in all thy ways acknowledge him, and he shall direct thy paths."

16

Essentials of Prayer

One of the greatest privileges we have is prayer. When the disciples saw Jesus at prayer, they said to Him, "Lord, teach us to pray." You and I were taught prayers when we were children, and now we need to be taught how to pray. Prayer is much more than words from the lips; prayer is the expression of the desires of the heart. John Bunyan said, "When you pray, rather let your heart be without words than your words without heart." The Bible contains many prayer promises, but I'd like us to consider just one—John 15:7: "If ye abide in me, and my words abide in you, ye shall ask what ye will, and it shall be done unto you."

The disciples were broken-hearted. Jesus had met with them in the upper room, and He had told them that He was going to leave them. For three years He had taught them, guided them, protected them, even fed them, and now He was leaving them. In that last message before the cross, Jesus explained to them how He would care for them from heaven; and one of His promises was that He would answer their prayers. In the wonderful promise of John 15:7 there are three factors involved—abiding, asking, and answering.

At least a dozen times in John 15, Jesus uses this word *abide*. His illustration is that of a vine and its branches. The branches are united to the vine and draw upon its life and strength. All the branch has to do is abide, stay in contact with the vine, and it will bear fruit. You and I as Christians are united by Christ to the faith. But along with this union there must be communion; we must fellowship with Christ and draw upon His life and power. To abide in Christ simply means to keep in fellowship with Him; and this we do through the Word of God, worship, and obedience. If we disobey Him, we break the fellowship, and we cannot pray. But if we obey Him and allow His Word to control our lives, then we can pray and God will answer.

This abiding has two sides to it: we abide in Christ and His Word abides in us. If you and I spend time every day in the Word of God, then we can talk to God about our needs and ask Him for His help. When I open my Bible, God talks to me. When I pray, I talk to God. It is far more important that I listen to God than He listen to me! One of the secrets of answered prayer is abiding in the Word and letting the Word abide in you. Spending time in the reading of the Bible is like spending time conversing with a dear friend.

It is tragic to see how many Christians neglect fellowship with the Lord. They rush into each new day without taking time to read the Bible or talk to God. Then they wonder why problems develop and why God doesn't answer their prayers.

The second factor involved in prayer is *asking*. "If ye abide in me and my words abide in you, ye shall ask what ye will and it shall be done unto you." Prayer is much more than asking; it also involves praising God, giving thanks, worshiping Him and surrendering to Him. But asking is an important part of praying. Jesus said, "Ask and it shall be given you." And James wrote, "Ye have not because ye ask not."

What right do we have to ask Almighty God for anything? Isn't it a bit presumptuous for a weak human being to ask the God of the universe for something? There are two answers to that question. To begin with, we are not just "weak human beings"; *we are children of God through faith in Jesus Christ*. Jesus once said, "If you, being evil, know how to give good gifts to your children, how much more shall your Father in heaven give good things to them that ask him?'' God hears the requests of His children. Peter wrote, ''The eyes of the Lord are upon the righteous, and his ears are open unto their cries. . . .''

When I was a child, the neighborhood children always gathered at our house. I can remember times when there were fifteen or more children on our porch or in our yard. My mother and father heard the racket, but their ears were especially tuned to the voices of their own four children. So it is with God. He hears the voices of nature, according to the psalmist—the beasts and birds when they cry out for food. And God hears the voices of the nations in rebellion. But above all the strife of voices in this world, God hears the cries of His own children. We have a right to ask God for what we need because we are His children through faith in Jesus Christ.

But there is a second reason why we have the right to pray: *God has invited us to pray.* In fact, He has commanded us. He knows that we cannot succeed in life unless we pray, so He has encouraged us to pray. You would think that we would rejoice at the privilege; yet somehow we get careless and forget to ask Him for what we need.

Abide in Christ, and then ask for what you need. Prayer is worship; prayer is praise and thanksgiving; but prayer is primarily asking God for what we need. If we abide in Him, and His words abide in us, then we will know what to ask for, and we will not pray selfishly or foolishly. If we neglect the abiding, then we are sure to fail in the asking. Spend time talking to God. Tell Him your needs, your problems, your heart's desires; and ask Him to give you what He knows is best. If you abide in Him, you can ask what you will and God will answer, because the right kind of abiding will lead to the right kind of asking.

Answering is the third aspect of prayer in John 15:7. God enjoys answering prayer, just as we parents enjoy meeting

the needs of our children when they ask us. John Newton
wrote in one of his hymns:

> Thou art coming to a king,
> Large petitions with thee bring;
> For His grace and power are such
> · None can ever ask too much.

You can imagine those discouraged disciples in that upper
room listening to Jesus talk to them about prayer. Up to then
they had never really had to pray. Jesus was right there with
them and they could turn to Him immediately with their
problems. But now He was leaving them, and He promises to
meet their needs if they will but abide and ask.

Archbishop Trench said that prayer is not overcoming
God's reluctance, but laying hold of His willingness. As
children, we learned quickly how to approach our parents to
ask for what we needed. We discovered that there were some
things we must never ask for because they were sure to say
no. So it is with God: as we ask Him for what He has promised to give us, He answers our prayers and meets the need.
This is why the Bible is so important in praying—it tells us
what God wants to give us. The Bible is our spiritual bank-
book, and our prayers are the checks we write, drawing upon
God's infinite resources.

Perhaps the most difficult problem in praying is the problem of delay. We tell God our needs, we trust Him to work,
and yet nothing seems to be happening. God knows how and
when to answer prayer. God's clock never needs winding or
resetting—He always knows what time it is. It has well been
said, "God's delays are not God's denials." God's ways are
not our ways, and He knows what is best.

As you determine to pray, start with the abiding and allow
the Word of God to get into your heart and purify you. Then
do the asking—tell God what is on your heart. Leave the
matter with Him and He will take care of the answering in
His good time.

17

Strength to Keep Going

One of the great men of history is the prophet Isaiah. He ministered to his people at a time when the nation was suffering from decay within and invasion without. He saw the coming of the great Babylonian armies and knew that they would destroy Jerusalem, take his people captive, and leave the nation in ruin. But in the midst of all of this confusion and discouragement, Isaiah received a message from God. It was a message of hope and encouragement for his suffering people: "They that wait upon the Lord shall renew their strength; they shall mount up with wings as eagles; they shall run, and not be weary; and they shall walk, and not faint." This is a promise for people who are ready to quit.

There are times when life becomes difficult and we feel like quitting. Everything presses in around us, and the future looks dark. Instead of facing the day with excitement and eager expectation, we face the day with weariness and depression. We are ready to faint. When some people get to this difficult experience of life, they turn to some substitute—drink or dope or entertainment—only to discover that these things can never carry them through. Some discouraged, fainting people even think of taking their own lives.

In the difficult hours of life, when you feel like fainting and giving up, turn to this mangnificent promise from Isaiah 40:31. Let's consider what it means to us today.

First of all, God promises *to help us fly*. There are times in our lives when the only solution is to fly—to rise above the problems of life and soar over them. God wants to make eagles out of us, but sometimes we prefer to crawl like ants. What a tragedy! God is able to lift you above those difficult circumstances that have trapped you. This doesn't mean you ignore them or forget them; it means that you rise above them and get a heavenly perspective. The eagle is able to fly miles up in the sky—and when you do that, the things on earth start to look much smaller. Yes, my friend, God promises to make you fly.

Of course, if you don't know Christ as your Savior, you cannot claim this wonderful promise. If that's the case, then your first step is to bow before Him and give your heart to Him by faith. Then you can ask God to make you fly, and He will lift you above and give you victory.

God not only promises to make us fly, but He also promises *to help us run*. All of us know what it is to be weary. There are times when we just have to keep running, crisis hours when we simply cannot quit. Perhaps you work all day and then spend time visiting a loved one in a hospital or caring for a friend and then go back home to care for responsibilities there; and on it goes, day after day. It is then that God promises to give us the strength to run and not be weary.

Doctors tell us that the emergency hours of life release in our bodies strength that we never knew we had. Our glands go to work and put extra power into the bloodstream, and we are able to do amazing things. If this is true physically, it is even more true spiritually. In the emergency hours of life, when we are sure we cannot keep going, God enables us to run and not be weary. We just keep going and accomplish the purposes God has in our lives.

But there is a third promise here: God promises to help us fly and to help us run, but He also promises *to help us walk*. "They shall walk and not faint." Frankly, I think it is more difficult to keep on walking than it is to fly. Somehow during those crisis hours of life we turn to the Lord and find His power to help us soar above the problems. There is a special excitement and challenge about the emergencies of life; but what about the full daily routine of life? It is one thing to mount up with wings as the eagle, or to run and not be weary—but what about walking, walking, walking, day after day?

A friend of mine had a maid who often came up with choice sayings. She said to my friend one day, "You know, the trouble with life is that it's so daily." Well, it is daily—day after day, life comes to us—but God has promised to give us the strength we need each day so that we can walk and not faint. There may not be anything romantic about your daily routine, but it is important to you, to God, and to others who depend on you.

God can help you fly, run, and walk, but there is something you must do. Isaiah 40:31 says, "They that *wait* upon the Lord shall renew their strength. . . ." Waiting on the Lord is the secret of keeping going when you feel like quitting.

What does it mean to wait on the Lord? First of all, we must spend time in His presence in worship and prayer. You and I are prone to be impulsive and rush ahead of God. If only we would wait on the Lord and remain quiet in His presence, we would get the wisdom and strength we need to keep going day after day. "Wait on the Lord," says the psalmist, "be of good courage, and he shall strengthen your heart; wait, I say, on the Lord." What a difference it makes when we quiet our hearts before God, read His Word, talk to Him in prayer, and wait patiently for His strength.

That word *renew* in Isaiah 40:31 actually means "exchange." "They that wait upon the Lord shall exchange their strength. . . ." We exchange our strength for His strength. We hand in our little pocket batteries and plug into His dynamo! He has all the strength we need to keep going, and there is no reason for us to quit. If you are considering giving up, please take time to consider the promise in Isaiah 40:31. Wait before the Lord, and let Him quiet you down. Exchange your weakness for His strength and spend time before Him every day. You will be amazed at the changes that will take place. Instead of fainting, you will be flying—you will mount up with wings as the eagle; you will run and not be weary; you will walk and not faint.

18

Victory over Fear

A lady once approached D. L. Moody and told him she had found a wonderful promise in the Bible that helped her overcome fear. Her verse was Psalm 56:3: "What time I am afraid, I will trust in thee." Mr. Moody replied, "Why I have a better promise than that!" And he quoted Isaiah 12:2: "Behold, God is my salvation; I will trust, and not be afraid." Mr. Moody did have a greater promise.

These words from Isaiah 12:2 are worth knowing in these days when it is so easy to become frightened. Jesus told us that in the end times men's hearts will fail them for fear of the things about to happen; and I believe we are seeing some of this take place today. Psychologists are writing books and magazine articles about overcoming fear.

There are some kinds of fear that are good for us. We warn our children not to go near the busy streets, and we put within them a healthy fear of being struck by a car. Eventually, of course, that infantile fear will be replaced by mature common sense; but until that happens, we dare not take any chances. In fact, the fear of punishment is one basis for discipline. It may not be the highest motive for doing good, but at least it helps us to get started.

The Bible often talks about the fear of the Lord. It tells us that the "fear of the Lord is the beginning of knowledge" and that "the fear of the Lord is a fountain of life." This fear, of course, is a proper respect and reverence for God. It is not the cringing fear of a slave before a brutal master, but the proper respect of a son before a loving Father. It is the kind of fear that opens the way to abundant life in Christ.

The kind of fear Isaiah 12:2 is talking about is the fear that paralyzes people—the fear that gets into the heart and mind and creates tension and worry, and that keeps a person from enjoying life and doing his best. I meet people every week who are afraid of life, afraid of death, afraid of the past, afraid of the future—in fact, people whose lives are being enslaved by fear.

Jesus Christ never meant for us to be the slaves of fear. It is exciting to read the Bible and discover how many times God says "Fear not" to people. When the angels appeared to the shepherds to announce the birth of Christ at Bethlehem, their first words were, "Fear not." When Peter fell at Jesus' feet and asked Jesus to depart from him because Peter felt he was a sinful man, Jesus said, "Fear not, Peter." When Jairus received the bad news that his daughter had just died, Jesus said to Jairus, "Fear not, only believe. . . ." Jesus Christ wants us to conquer fear; and He is able to help us win the battle.

What causes fear in our lives? Sometimes fear is caused by a *guilty conscience*. When Adam and Eve sinned, they felt guilty and became afraid; and they tried to hide from God. Shakespeare was right when he said, "Conscience doth make cowards of us all." Whenever we disobey God, we lose our close fellowship with Him, and that spiritual loneliness creates fear. We wonder if anybody knows what we have done. We worry about being found out, and hope no tragic consequences come from our sins. The solution to that problem, of course, is to seek God's forgiveness. God promises to cleanse our sins if we will but confess them and forsake them.

Often fear is caused by *ignorance*. Children are afraid in the night because the shadows look like giants and bears and ghosts. But even adults can get frightened when they really don't know what is going on. Fear of the future, either for ourselves or for our loved ones, can sometimes create fear. Another cause is *our own feeling of weakness*. We are so accustomed to managing things ourselves, that when an unmanageable crisis comes along, we feel helpless and afraid.

Sometimes fear comes, not before the battle or even in the midst of the battle, but after we have won the victory. Often there is an emotional let down, and fear rushes in. Abraham had this experience in Genesis 14 after he had waged war against four powerful kings and won the victory. That night as he lay down to sleep Abraham wondered if those kings would return and challenge him again, and perhaps bring back superior forces. It was then that God appeared to Abraham and said, "Fear not, Abraham; I am thy shield and thy exceeding great reward."

But when we study all the cases and try to understand the root cause of fear, one truth stands out clearly: *the real cause of fear is unbelief*. After stilling a storm that had frightened His disciples out of their wits, Jesus said to them, "Why are you so fearful? How is it that you have no faith?" Fear and faith can never be friends; and if we are afraid, it is a sign that we have no faith. This is why Isaiah 12:2 says, "Behold, God is my salvation; I will trust, and not be afraid."

The secret of victory over fear is faith in God. There is no problem too great for God to solve, no burden too heavy for God to carry, no battle too overwhelming for God to fight and win. God is big enough to conquer the enemies that rob us of our peace and leave paralyzing fears behind. Isaiah 12:2 doesn't say, "When I am afraid, I will trust," it says, "I will trust and not be afraid." Faith is not simply medicine to kill the disease; faith is spiritual power to keep us from being infected in the first place.

Notice what the prophet puts first: "Behold God is my salvation." If you want to overcome fear, get your eyes off yourself and your feelings, and off the problems that have upset you and get your eyes on God. The Jewish spies in the Old Testament became frightened when they investigated the Promised Land, because they saw giants and high walls and felt like grasshoppers in comparison. The enemy soldiers *were* big, and the walls *were* high, but God was far above all of them. Had the spies lifted their eyes just a bit higher and seen God, they would not have been afraid. So the first step in overcoming fear is to *look by faith at God*. Worship God, get a fresh glimpse of His greatness and glory, and realize that He is still on the throne. The second step is to *lay hold of God's Word*. Faith comes by hearing, and hearing by the Word of God. When you read the Bible, you find your faith growing. You discover that God has always been adequate for the needs of His people.

The third step is to *pray and surrender to the Holy Spirit*. Tell God about your fears—tell Him that your fears are really evidences of unbelief—and like that concerned man in the Gospel story, ask God to help your unbelief. Surrender yourself to the Holy Spirit of God, because the Spirit can work in you to take away fear and give you peace. II Timothy 1:7 says, "For God has not given us the spirit of fear; but of power, and of love, and of a sound mind." The Holy Spirit within you can give you power for your weakness; He can generate love; He can give order and discipline to your mind. The Holy Spirit is God's psychologist, so turn yourself over to Him.

One of the ministries of the Spirit of God is making Jesus Christ real to us. As you pray and read the Word, the Spirit will give you a spiritual understanding of Jesus Christ, and He will become very real to you. Even in the midst of storms and trials, Jesus Christ comes with peace and courage for you.

There is not reason for you to be afraid. Fear will only rob you and buffet you and paralyze you. Jesus Christ can take away your fear and give you peace. "Behold, God is my salvation; I will trust and not be afraid.

19

The Weaver's Shuttle

Centuries ago a Roman poet penned two famous words: "Time flies." But a person doesn't have to be a poet or a philosopher to know that time is always passing. Another poet has said, "Time goes you say? Ah, no—time stays, we go!" And perhaps he is right. The Bible has much to say about time and the fact that time is swiftly passing. Let's look at Job 7:6: "My days are swifter than a weaver's shuttle, and are spent without hope."

The older we get, the faster time seems to move. It seems that as soon as we have finished the Christmas shopping we are packing for summer vacation. Then the children go back to school and before we know it, the holidays are back again. As I fill out my datebook month by month, I marvel that time is moving so rapidly. Of course, for some people, time seems to creep; but for most of us, Job's words are applicable.

My wife and I often vacationed in a quiet mountain town that had several shops devoted to mountain crafts. It was delightful to walk through the mills and watch the weavers at work on the old-fashioned looms. If Job thought the hand looms of his day were fast, he should see what we have today! That shuttle zooms through the webbing and comes back again so fast you can hardly see it. Job has picked out a good picture of the swiftness of human life.

The fact that life is moving so rapidly these days has created some new problems. For one thing, you and I don't have the time to understand and accept things the way our parents and grandparents did years ago. Today when something happens, the whole world knows about it within a few minutes; and so much is happening that we are being bombarded with news and changes and threats. One writer calls this "future shock." Doctors tell us that people are actually becoming emotionally and physically ill because of the stress of life and the rapidity of change.

There are several ways to handle this problem. One is to retreat into the past and let the world go its merry way. But Christians can't do that. We have a ministry to this world, and we can't stop the world and get off. Nostalgia for the good old days is fun for a while, and there is nothing wrong with it, but nostalgia can never be a way of life for the dedicated Christian. Another possible approach is to fight change and try to slow down the shuttle, but this approach is doomed to failure. You might just as well try to stop a jet plane with a slingshot as to slow down the forces of change in today's world.

No, the Christian has to live a life in the context of a real world; and he must trust Christ to give him the peace and strength he needs day by day. God isn't affected by time and change; He is the great I Am. Jesus Christ is the same yesterday, today, and forever. God's Word is forever settled in heaven. Heaven and earth may pass away, but His Word will never pass away. So if life is moving too fast for you, don't fight it and don't give in to it. Instead, surrender to Christ and let time work for you and not against you.

"My days are swifter than a weaver's shuttle." Job was going through some rough times when he made that statement, so it is no wonder he added, "and they are spent without hope." Job's situation did look pretty hopeless. He had lost his wealth and his family in a series of tragic events. Then he lost his health. Everything around him was falling apart, and he could see no light in the darkness. When he tried to reach God, it seemed that even God was far away.

When I am ill or when I am going through difficulties, time seems to stand still. I can recall times when I was recuperating in the hospital when the days just trudged along like tired turtles, and I wanted them to speed along like locomotives. Job was a sick man, and his situation was difficult, yet he complained that his days were moving too fast for him. In fact, that whole seventh chapter of the Book of Job deals with the swiftness of human life. Job compares his life to a wind and a cloud that are here one minute and gone the next. In the next two chapters he pictures his life as a shadow, or a ship that appears and then is gone. It is a flower that blooms and fades.

But perhaps Job saw some good in the swiftness of life. First, since life is moving rapidly, our circumstances will change. We don't know how many days are involved in the story of Job, but we do know that one day God appeared on the scene, and Job ended up in better condition than he started.

Second, since our lives are like a weaver's shuttle, there is a pattern and a purpose involved. God controls the shuttle and God has a pattern for our lives. This ought to encourage us no matter how difficult the days may be. As long as God is on the throne, there is hope!

Did you ever look on the wrong side of the loom? There is really nothing beautiful about it. After the work is completed, the weaver takes the work off the loom and cuts off the extra threads and puts the finishing touches on the blanket or sweater or whatever he was weaving.

You and I are still on the loom. God isn't finished with us yet. As you and I look at the process, we see the shuttle running swiftly through the web, and we see some kind of a pattern developing; but only the weaver can see the finished product. Never judge the weaver by an unfinished product. Don't get angry at God because you don't agree with His choice of colors or patterns. You and I cannot see the total picture; only God can see that. And don't get disgusted with life because the pattern isn't what you want. The weaver knows best. Some people try to improve the pattern, and they end up making it ugly instead of beautiful.

And never judge another person's life or give up on him. You may be a parent, discouraged over your wayward children; or perhaps you are a pastor or missionary who is weeping over people who are rebelling against God. Let the divine Weaver handle the situation. What looks to us today as a marred product can, in Christ's hands, become a beautiful weaving. He can untangle the threads; He can untie the knots; and He can weave life together so that the finished product brings honor to His name. Just keep praying and trusting, and let the Weaver do the rest.

Yes, life is swifter than a weaver's shuttle; but I'm not afraid. The Weaver has everything under control and He is weaving our lives according to His perfect plan. Sometimes we get discouraged because all we can see is the wrong side of the weaving. But God sees both sides, and He is working all things together for your good and His glory. When time finally ends, and the shuttle is at rest; when the Weaver takes the weaving off the loom; then you and I will understand just why He wove the design as He did. And when we understand, we will fall down and praise Him for His wisdom and goodness.

Help, Hope, and Happiness

20

I was paging through an old Bible of mine one day and discovered a note I had written in the margin on August 13, 1957. At that time I was sharing an evangelistic mission in Denmark, and the going was really tough. The verse I had marked was Psalm 146:5: "Happy is he that hath the God of Jacob for his help, whose hope is in the Lord his God." I'm sure that verse gave me great encouragement for that day, because it promises everything that the Christian needs—help, hope, and happiness. This verse is like those charts on the back of cereal boxes that list the minimum daily requirements for health. Here we have the minimum daily requirements for spiritual health—help, hope, and happiness.

"Happy is he that hath the God of Jacob for his help. . . ." No matter how capable and efficient you and I may be, there come times when we need help. I have no mechanical ability, so I have to depend on the help of the garage mechanic whenever my car needs servicing. I try to take care of my health, but there have been times when the expert help of the physician or surgeon has been needed. You and I depend on the help of others all day long—the people who manage the telephone circuits, the workers who keep the busses and trains operating, the people who print the newspaper.

But there is One whose help is far above all, and that One

is the God of Jacob. God can do for us what nobody else can do. Psalm 46:1 tells us that God is "a very present help in trouble." The psalmist said, "My help cometh from the Lord which made heaven and earth." You and I trust people, yet people fail us; and we sometimes fail others. But when we put our trust in the Lord, He gives the kind of help that never fails.

God is called here "the God of Jacob," and this is a great encouragement to me because Jacob was always needing help. When he tricked his brother and father and had to leave home, Jacob was all alone in an unfriendly world. Yet God protected him and directed him and met his every need. When other men tried to hurt Jacob, God stepped in to shelter him. God fulfilled His purposes for Jacob and made him the father of the tribes of Israel. Jacob was sometimes a disobedient man, but God still helped him and saw him through.

So here is a word of encouragement for us today: The God of Jacob is our help. Hebrews 13:6 reads, "The Lord is my helper, and I will not fear what man shall do unto me." Cast your burden on the Lord, and by faith, receive the help that He alone can give. "God is our refuge and strength, a very present help in time of trouble."

We've looked at the help that God gives us; now let's think about hope. Sad to say, there are multitudes of people who have no hope. They have nothing to live for, nothing to look forward to. Often I receive frantic phone calls from people who are about to end it all; life has become unbearable for them, and they would rather die than live.

When you know Jesus Christ, you always have hope. Paul tells us that Jesus Christ is our hope! To the Christian, hope is not a mirage or a blind optimism. Our hope in Christ is a certainty. Hebrews 6:19 tells us that our hope in Christ is an anchor. And that anchor will never slip or never fail. The Christian "rejoices in hope" because he knows that the future is secure in Christ.

Our hope in Christ is based on the Word of God, the Bible. Because we trust His promises, we experience His hope. No matter how dark the day may become, we still have the light of His Word to encourage us. Ferdinand Magellan took thirty-five compasses with him when he started on his voyage around the world. A ship without a compass is doomed—and so is a life without hope. The Word of God is the light that encourages us and the compass that guides us.

Of course, if you have never trusted Christ as your Savior, you have no hope. It is only when you surrender to Him that hope comes into your heart. The Christian never has to lose hope because he has a Savior to walk with Him into the future. Even when you walk through the valley of the shadow of death you will not be afraid, because Jesus will be right there with you. When you know Him, you have help and you have hope, so that the present and the future are all taken care of. No wonder the Christian experiences happiness: "Happy is he that hath the God of Jacob for his help, whose hope is in the Lord his God." What is happiness? We have many clever and shallow definitions of happiness these days. But to the mature person, happiness is much deeper than what these juvenile definitions describe. Happiness is that wonderful feeling of well-being that comes when we are depending on God's help and living in God's will. If we are depending on our own help, ultimately we will fail; and if we are living for our own will, we can never really be happy.

Happiness is a by-product. If you look for happiness, you will never find it; but if you determine to trust Christ and obey Him, then happiness will come your way. You can't purchase happiness or store it away. Jesus said, "A man's life does not consist in the abundance of the things that he possesses." In fact, some of the most miserable people I know are depending on their accumulated wealth. Happiness is never found in things.

Nor is happiness found in thrills, for thrills never last. I thank God for happy memories, and I treasure them, but

God doesn't want us to face life looking in a rear-view mirror.

What is it you need right now? Do you need help? "Happy is he that hath the God of Jacob for his help. . ." says Psalm 146:5. Do you need hope? "Happy is he that hath the God of Jacob for his help, whose hope is in the Lord his God." And when you have God's help and hope, you will experience His happiness as well. You will have help for today and hope for tomorrow because you trust Christ; and you will have happiness in your heart as a blessed by-product of God's grace.

21

The Eternal Encourager

If ever a group of people felt as though their world had collapsed, it was the disciples in the upper room. Jesus told them that one of them would betray Him to the enemy and that Peter would deny Him. Then He told them that He was leaving them to return to His Father in heaven. Was there any encouragement or hope for these men? Yes, there was; for Jesus promised them, "And I will pray the Father, and He shall give you another Comforter, that He may abide with you for ever" (John 14:16). He was speaking, of course, of the Holy Spirit of God who lives within the heart of each believer.

We use the word *comforter* to mean "someone who sympathizes, someone who feels our hurts with us." But the word has a much deeper meaning than that. I could sympathize with you and perhaps never really help you. The word translated "Comforter" in our New Testament really means "to call to one's side." Perhaps the best translation would be "the encourager." The Holy Spirit is our encourager and He is always with us to help us live for Christ.

Our English word *comfort* comes from two Latin words: *com* means "with" and *fort* means "strength." So a comforter is not somebody who pats us on the shoulder and says, "Keep your chin up!" but someone who helps to give us the strength we need to keep going.

Jesus told His disciples that the Father would send them "another Comforter," and that word *another* means "another of the same kind." The Spirit of God takes the place of the Son of God. He is equal to the Son and able to encourage us just as Jesus encouraged His disciples. I have heard Christians say, "If Jesus Christ were right here with me as He was with His disciples, then I would be a better Christian!" That is a poor excuse. To begin with, even though Jesus was with His disciples, they often failed Him. And Jesus Christ is with us by His Spirit in a far deeper way than He ever was with His disciples when He was here on earth. The Holy Spirit dwells in us, and He is to us what Jesus was to His disciples.

What did Jesus do for His disciples? He taught them His Word, and the Holy Spirit is our teacher to show us the truths of the Bible. Jesus gave His disciples directions concerning God's will, and the Holy Spirit leads us in the will of God. Our Lord occasionally had to convict His disciples and deal with their sin, and the indwelling Holy Spirit has to convict us when we have disobeyed. The Savior gave His disciples the power they needed for service, and the Holy Spirit gives us the power we need to be workers and witnesses for the Lord. It is impossible to live a joyful, successful Christian life without the Holy Spirit of God.

I meet many discouraged Christians these days. Some are discouraged because of circumstances, problems of one kind or another. Others are discouraged because of failure; people have failed them, or they feel as though they have failed God. Many people have to live with pain and handicaps of one kind or another, and this is always an opportunity for discouragement. Christian workers get discouraged because they feel their work is in vain and they are accomplishing very little for God. Yes, these are days when many people are discouraged.

But the Holy Spirit is our encourager. To be sure, He will discourage us from sinning, but He will never discourage us in our service or our Christian living. The Father sent the Holy Spirit to be our encourager, so if you are discouraged, it may be because you are not depending on the Holy Spirit of God.

How does the Holy Spirit encourage us as Christians? For one thing, He teaches us the truths of the Bible. Whenever I find myself getting tired and discouraged, I turn to the Bible and ask the Spirit to enlighten me, and He always does. He shows me the promises of the Word. He reveals God to me, and when I see how great God is, my own problems and burdens become very small. One of the great joys of the Christian life is to study God's Word and let the Holy Spirit reveal Christ to us. If you read your Bible without the aid of the Spirit, you will never receive any encouragement. But if you ask the Spirit of God to open your eyes to God's truth, the Comforter will teach you and encourage you.

The Holy Spirit encourages us in another way. He prays for us and helps us to pray in God's will. Romans 8:26 tells us that the Spirit of God intercedes for us, and that He prays in the will of God. We don't hear Him praying, but He prays for us, says Paul, "with groanings which cannot be uttered." I have friends who pray for me, but they cannot pray for me constantly. Yet the Holy Spirit, who lives in me, prays for me constantly, and this is an encouragement to me.

Third, the Holy Spirit gives us the power we need to live the Christian life. "For it is God that worketh in you, both to will and to do of his good pleasure" (Phil. 2:13). Whatever spiritual power we need, the Spirit is there to grant it. Do you need patience to endure a difficult situation? The Spirit is there to grant it. Do you need courage to face a dangerous challenge? The Spirit of God can give you that courage. As you read the Word, and as you yield to the Spirit, He will enable you to accomplish the will of God, no matter how weak and ineffective you may feel.

Finally, the Spirit of God takes away fear. "For God has not given us the spirit of fear; but of power, and of love, and of a sound mind" (II Tim. 1:7). The early church faced, in the power of the Spirit, a wicked and hostile world, and they had no fear. When the Spirit of God fills you and controls you, there is an inner peace and confidence that drives away fear. Fear always destroys faith; fear always takes away strength. But when you have the Spirit of God encouraging you, there is no need to be afraid.

The principal reason why the Holy Spirit is in the world today is to glorify the Son of God. Jesus said of the Spirit, "He shall glorify me." The Spirit of God did not come to glorify men or churches or organizations; He came to glorify Jesus Christ. If you and I are living for the glory of God, then the Spirit of God will encourage us and enable us to serve Christ. But if we are looking for the glory, then we will grieve the Spirit. It is a dangerous thing to try to control the Holy Spirit and tell Him what He can do in our lives. We need never fear what the Spirit of God will do, for He loves us and wants the very best for our lives. The Spirit always obeys the Word of God and will never lead you out of the will of God.

If you find yourself discouraged and ready to quit, take time to examine your relationship to the Holy Spirit. Are you fully yielded to Him? Are you grieving Him by unconfessed sin? Are you quenching Him by willful disobedience? Have you been neglecting your Bible and prayer? These are the usual causes of spiritual defeat and discouragement, and we need to make things right when we discover they are wrong.

But suppose you are obeying the Lord and seeking to glorify Christ, and you are still under a cloud of discouragement? What then? Yield to the Spirit and trust Him to work matters out in His good time. Feed on the Word of God. Do not permit yourself to give in to your feelings, or to judge God's promises by the difficult circumstances around you. The Spirit of God is not distant from you, sending you advice; He is living in you and giving you the strength and wisdom you need for the decisions of life. Trust Him, wait for

His help, and know that He will never fail you. In due time, the Comforter will minister to your needs and encourage your heart.

22

Big Lessons from Little Things

You and I are too impressed with size. If something is small and quiet, we have the idea that it is unimportant; but if it is big and noisy, then it must be important. But God doesn't measure life the way we do. The big things don't always impress Him. In fact, some of the little things in the Bible teach big lessons.

The prophet Zechariah asked an interesting question one day: "For who has despised the day of small things?" He was trying to encourage the nation as they were rebuilding their temple and having a difficult time. The budget was low, the morale even lower, and it looked like the job would never be finished. The people were discouraged because the whole project seemed so small—it just wasn't the temple it used to be.

We had better be careful not to despise small things! After all, we got our start in this world as babies, totally dependent on others. When God wanted to deliver His people from Egypt, He didn't send an army—He sent a baby to a Jewish family, and years later, Moses led his people out of bondage. When the nation had sunk into spiritual and political defeat, God sent a boy named Samuel who one day led the nation back into greatness. And when God wanted to deliver mankind from sin, He sent another baby. Jesus Christ came as a baby that He might one day die for us on the cross.

God uses small things to accomplish great purposes. He used Moses' rod to defeat the armies of Egypt. He used David's sling to overcome the giant Goliath. Gideon and his three hundred soldiers used pitchers and torches to slaughter the huge army of the Midianites. Rahab tied a piece of red rope out of her window, and it saved her family. A lad brought a few loaves and fishes to Jesus, and He used them to feed thousands. Never despise the small things because God can use them to accomplish great things.

You may think that you are insignificant in the great plan of God, but you are not. You are tremendously important to God—so much so that Jesus died for you, and the Holy Spirit lives in you. You may seem small in your own eyes, and this is good; because God resists the proud but gives grace to the humble. However, don't let your humility become sin by making you believe you can do nothing for God. God can use you to help Him accomplish His will on this earth.

God not only uses small things, but God uses small acts that seem insignificant to us and to others. How many times have you done something good and thought, "Well, nobody knows about that and it won't accomplish much." How wrong you are! There is no deed of sacrifice or kindness that goes unnoticed by God. He can use these small deeds of Christian love and accomplish great things.

I think, for example, of what Mary of Bethany did for Jesus. Shortly before His death on the cross, Jesus and His disciples were having supper at the home of Mary and Martha and Lazarus. Mary came into the room with a jar of expensive perfume, and she poured it out on Jesus' feet as a loving act of worship. Nobody outside that house knew what she did. In fact, some inside the house criticized her for doing it. But Jesus defended her and made an amazing statement: "Wherever this gospel shall be preached throughout the whole world, this also that she has done shall be spoken of for a memorial to her." This one act of worship had worldwide effects!

Whatever is done in love for Christ will have power and influence for all eternity. The widow brought to the temple just two mites, worth less than an American penny; yet Jesus said she gave more than all the rich people put together, and her act of worship has been a blessing to people around the world for many centuries. No sincere act of worship or service is overlooked by God. Men may despise small things, but God encourages them; it is in the small things that a person's faithfulness is really seen. Many people would have no problem participating in a big event in public; but how many are willing to serve God and worship Him in the little place where nobody is watching?

The Christian who can't be trusted with the small things can never be trusted with the big things! Jesus tells us that if we are faithful in that which is least we will also be faithful in that which is greatest. To Him, the least is the greatest because it leads to the greatest. All of which means that you and I had better examine our values and our priorities lest we be found despising the day of small things.

When God asks, "Who has despised the day of small things?" He is not suggesting that things stay small. The church began with 120 faithful praying people in the upper room, and within a few weeks numbered over five thousand people. Had the believers despised their small group, they would never have become a large church. A man asked me one day, "How big do you think a church ought to be?" I replied, "As big as it deserved to be." God wants His church to grow; He certainly wants to see people saved from sin. In John 15, Jesus talks about "fruit . . . more fruit . . . much fruit." He said, "Herein is my Father glorified, that ye bear much fruit."

Faithfulness in the small things will lead to blessing in the big things. David proved himself faithful in taking care of his father's sheep, so God gave him a whole nation to shepherd. David trusted God in private as he killed the lion and the bear, so God let him kill the giant in public. Timothy was faithful as Paul's helper, and one day he became Paul's successor. If we are faithful in the small things, God will trust us with the bigger things if this is His will.

But there is a warning here: *not everything that is big is necessarily of God.* It is possible for us to manufacture success in our own way and discover that God is not in the earthquake or the wind. The tower of Babel was a great success until God sent His judgment and the whole thing fell apart. Perhaps some of us are building modern towers of Babel and the judgment is around the corner.

Since God uses the small things, *never be influenced by the evaluations of men.* I enjoy reading biography, and I am amazed to see how the most successful men and women were ridiculed and rejected when they first started their work. William Carey was opposed by preachers when he tried to get a missionary agency started. Hudson Taylor was laughed at when he dared to go alone to China without the guarantee of support from home. When D. L. Moody started his little meetings in England, nobody dreamed they would turn into a tremendous force for God that moved two continents, and eventually touched the whole world. Men have a way of despising what is small, so be careful not to follow the ideas of men. Get your values from God.

Not all works are going to be big in the eyes of men and be known around the world. But that's not the important thing. The important thing is that we do our work well so that it will be big in the eyes of God. As those feeble Jews tried to rebuild their temple, their work looked pitifully small; but it was God's work just the same. And that temple would one day see the very Son of God standing in its courts, healing the sick, forgiving sinners, and teaching the multitudes. Never despise the day of small things. It is in the small things that God can work and bless; and the small things prepare for the bigger things.

No work is small if it is God's work. No gift is small if it is given in faith and love. No act of service is small if it is done to the glory of Christ. Don't go around comparing yourself with others. Let God do the measuring and the weighing. He measures for eternity—and that is what really counts.

23

Try Forgiveness

Recently I chatted with a man who was nervous, physically ill, and disturbed emotionally. I felt he should visit a specialist, but he wanted to talk with me, so I patiently listened. As his story came out, I began to understand why he was so miserable: he was long on memory and short on forgiveness. He remembered every unkind thing anybody had ever said or done to him. At times his eyes blazed with murderous anger. Once more I was reminded of the importance of forgiveness as one of the greatest spiritual medicines in all the world.

Mark Twain is best known for his humorous stories, but he could be a philosopher when he wanted to be. One of the most beautiful things he ever said was, "Forgiveness is the fragrance the violet sheds on the heel that crushed it." Forgiveness is not easy, but it is necessary. An unforgiving spirit doesn't hurt the other person; it hurts us. To harbor grudges, to cultivate malice toward another person, to refuse to forgive—all of these poison the inner man and produce spiritual and emotional sickness that no man-made medicines can cure.

I am amazed at the great number of disturbed people I meet who carry in their heart an unforgiving spirit. These people come to me with their problems—they are restless; they run from job to job or apartment to apartment, never able to settle down; they are always being hurt by somebody;

they have a hard time making friends. When I ask them if they have ever forgiven those who have wronged them, they look at me with a shocked expression as if I have read their minds. The symptoms are typical, and you and I can detect them in ourselves as well as in others.

When you have an unforgiving spirit, you think you are better than other people. They make mistakes, but you never make mistakes. When you have an unforgiving spirit, you are super-sensitive; you take very personally what other people say and do. You become suspicious of their motives and you feel that somebody is going to hurt you. An unforgiving spirit causes a person to withdraw into himself and become a spectator in life, not a participant. After all, when you are better than other people and they are out to get you, why get friendly? This explains why unforgiving people are usually lonely, critical, nervous people.

But one of the saddest results of an unforgiving spirit is the build up of aggression on the inside. Many people who carry grudges and harbor malice are filled with hostility. They are unable to laugh off the little problems that people sometimes cause; they take these matters seriously and build them into big issues. If somebody pushes ahead of them on the bus, they take it personally and declare war. If nobody really causes any trouble, the unforgiving people can usually imagine something and invent a problem to fight about.

In order to forgive, you have to be forgiven. When you experience the forgiveness of God in your own heart and realize that Jesus died for you, then you can begin to forgive others and rid your system of the poison of malice. But you can't be forgiven until you admit you need forgiveness, and that is where the rub comes in. Very few people like to admit they are sinners in need of God's gracious forgiveness. This explains why some people are always condemning others: by making others look bad, they think they can make themselves look good. And once they believe that they are that good, then they see no need for forgiveness.

I recall counseling with a lady who was gifted at finding fault with others. But she was unable to see any needs in her own life. Patiently I talked with her, and the longer we talked, the clearer it became to me that her judging of others was really a mask to hide herself. Finally I asked her if there was not some great disappointment in her life that pained her; and then she broke down and cried, admitting that there was. There was an old wound that she had never permitted God to heal. It had festered all those years and poisoned her system. Once she admitted it to herself, and then confessed it to God, it was healed. And once she was forgiven, she was able to forgive others.

This is what Paul meant when he wrote, "And be ye kind one to another, tenderhearted, forgiving one another, even as God for Christ's sake hath forgiven you." On the cross Jesus prayed, "Father, forgive them, for they know not what they do." Because He shed His blood, you and I can experience God's gracious forgiveness. There is no way we can earn His forgiveness; it is a gift. When you turn to Christ in faith, confess your need, and ask for His forgiveness, He grants it to you unconditionally. If He does all this for us, should we not be able to forgive others?

It is possible to receive forgiveness from God but not really experience it in our hearts. We know God has saved us, but it hasn't really registered deep within. It is sort of a commercial transaction that needs to become personal. We have the doctrine in our head but it needs to get to our heart. We know we are going to heaven, but somehow heaven hasn't come down to us and given us a forgiving spirit toward others. What can we do about this? How can a person cultivate a forgiving spirit and avoid the terrible poison of malice and hatred? By realizing what a great sinner he really is! Perhaps we aren't guilty of some of the gross sins that we see in other people, but we may have committed them in our hearts. At the end of his life, Paul called himself the "chief of sinners." The closer we get to the light, the dirtier our hearts and hands become. So the first suggestion I have for cultivating a forgiving spirit is to spend time daily with the Lord in His Word and in prayer. Get to know Him better. As you do, you will realize what sin really is, and you will discover that there are areas that still need help.

And as you fellowship daily with the Lord, you will discover how loving and gracious He is, and what it cost Him to forgive you. One reason why Jesus instituted the Lord's Supper was to remind us that He died for us. I cannot conceive of a person coming to the Lord's Table and going away with an unforgiving spirit. When we realize the meaning of the cross we have to forgive others.

Here is a third suggestion: let the Holy Spirit within you generate the kind of love that it takes to forgive others. The fruit of the Spirit is love. You and I cannot manufacture forgiveness; it is something God does within us as we yield to Him. Confess your unforgiving spirit to God; ask Him to forgive you and fill your heart with His love. Then go to those you have wronged and share God's love and forgiveness with them.

My last suggestion is a negative one, but I think it's important: realize how costly it is to have an unforgiving heart. Hannah More wrote, "A Christian will find it cheaper to pardon than to resent. Forgiveness saves the expense of anger, the cost of hatred, the waste of spirits." How true this is! If only people could see an x-ray of the inner man and realize the damage that is done when they harbor grudges and malice! No amount of compensation can repay you for an unforgiving spirit. Your enemy is not the one who suffers, you are.

It may take time, but start today to cultivate a spirit of forgiveness. Let God cleanse your heart and fill it with His love. The next time somebody offends you or hurts you, immediately forgive him from your heart. Resist every inclination to fight back, either on the outside or on the inside. Ask God to give you a gracious attitude, and treat that person with love. You will discover that forgiveness brings liberty and joy, while hatred creates misery and bondage. Day after day, the Holy Spirit will work in you and through you, and life will take on a different atmosphere for you and for those around you. "And be ye kind one to another, tenderhearted, forgiving one another, even as God for Christ's sake hath forgiven you."

24

Look at the Possibilities

One day Jesus visited a place in Jerusalem called "Bethesda" which means "house of grace." There were many sick people at that place because at certain times the water would be stirred, and whoever got into the water was healed. Jesus found a man there who had been crippled for thirty-eight years, and He asked the man, "Do you want to be healed?" Instead of saying "Yes, I do!" the man replied, "Sir, I have no man to put me in the water, and everybody else gets in before I do!" Before you criticize that man you had better ask yourself whether you have made the same mistake he made.

When Jesus showed up at the pool of Bethesda, and walked among those handicapped people waiting to be healed, He was bringing them the greatest opportunity they ever had. He was God—He was the Healer—and nobody had to struggle to the water to be healed. Faith in Christ would have healed them instantly.

This man who had been sick for thirty-eight years had been at the pool long enough to see others get into the moving waters and be healed. So day after day, year after year, he waited for his opportunity to come. But, alas, every time he tried to get into the water, nobody would help him, and somebody always got in before him. Jesus asked the man, "Do you want to be made whole?" Instead of replying,

"Yes, I do!" the man immediately began to complain about his sad situation. Little did he realize that the One who could change his situation was standing at His side.

That's the first mistake the crippled man made: *he judged the present by the past.* His argument was logical except for one thing: he left God out of the picture. God is not limited by the past. No matter how many disappointments and failures we may have had in the past, when Jesus Christ comes on the scene, everything has to change.

I can well understand the attitude of this man. When you have been shoved aside year after year and neglected by those who could help you, you get discouraged; and you come to the conclusion that you never will get any better. But this attitude was a mistake, Jesus Christ the Son of God was right by this man's side. He said to the man, "Rise—take up your bed and walk!" And the man obeyed by faith and was made whole!

Nothing paralyzes our lives like the attitude that things can never change. We need to remind ourselves that God can change things! God can forgive sin and put new power into lives that seem to be utter failures. God can send revival to a church that everybody thinks is dead. God can move into a difficult situation and turn seeming failure into victory. God makes the difference! And for us to judge the present by the past is to limit God.

The crippled man's second mistake was *seeing the problems and not the possibilities.* "Whenever the water is stirred and I try to get down, nobody will help me and somebody else always gets there first." But Jesus didn't ask the man what his problems were; he asked him what his desires were. "Do you want to be made whole?"

Perhaps this is what separates the optimist from the pessimist. The optimist sees possibilities in the problems, and the pessimist sees problems in the possibilities. One sees the opportunities and the other sees the obstacles. But the real basis for optimism is faith. When you bring God into the picture, even the greatest problems can become great potentials for blessing. The apostle Paul was a spiritual optimist. He wrote to his friends at Corinth from the city of Ephesus, "But I will tarry at Ephesus until Pentecost. For a great door and effectual is opened unto me, and there are many adversaries." You and I may have written, "In spite of the fact that there is a great opportunity here, I am leaving town because there are too many problems!"

Whether we like it or not, outlook determines outcome. If we see only the problems, we will be defeated; but if we see the possibilities in the problems, we can have victory. God took Moses' stammering lips and made the Bible's greatest orator out of him. He took Peter's misdirected courage and zeal and transformed him into a soul-winning preacher. And He took this crippled man at the pool of Bethesda and transformed him into a child of God with a witness to the glory of God. God can take any of us, no matter how discouraged and defeated we may be, and make out of us something wonderful for His glory.

One more mistake that this man made when Jesus met him at the pool of Bethesda was *seeing what he didn't have rather than what he did have.* God always starts with what we have before He gives us what we need. He took Moses' rod and David's sling and Peter's boat; and He can take what you have and use it to transform your life. What did this man have? A crippled body. But he also had faith to believe that he could be healed if he managed to get into the water. No doubt his faith got stronger every time he saw someone healed and weaker when he found himself left behind again. But he did have faith.

Faith is the one thing God requires if He is going to work miracles in our lives. The great heroes of the Bible were heroes, not because of their talents or personalities but because of their faith. If you have trusted Christ as your Savior, then you already have faith; and this faith has brought to you the greatest miracle of all—salvation. Now, instead of complaining about what you don't have, why not start with what you do have—your faith in Christ—and let that faith lay hold of the promises of God.

So often we overlook this tremendous thing called faith. We try to change situations in our own strength and wisdom, only to have the situations grow worse. If only we would turn ourselves and our problems over to the Lord, and trust Him to work, we would then discover what wonderful changes He can make. He said to some blind men one day, "According to your faith be it unto you" and He healed them. He says the same thing to you and me.

The man at the pool of Bethesda obeyed the command to stand up and walk. He had not stood and walked for thirty-eight years, but when the command of the Lord was given, he acted upon it by faith, and when he obeyed by faith, God's power went to work in his body and restored him. He could have argued, "But I can't stand up! I can't walk!" But faith never says "I can't"; faith says "God can!" "With God nothing is impossible!"

I'm sure that many people have situations that they would like to see changed. Perhaps you have been so wrapped up in the problems that you haven't been able to see the possibilities. You have gotten locked into the past and you can't realize that God is able to change the past. Jesus Christ comes to you now and asks whether or not you want to be made whole. You can respond with a complaint or an excuse and miss the miracle. Or you can respond with faith and experience the power of God. God may not give you an instant solution as he did the man at Bethesda, but He will begin to work in your life and lead you to the place of liberty and victory.

25

Three Treasures

"Now the God of hope fill you with all joy and peace in believing, that you may abound in hope through the power of the Holy Ghost." Paul wrote those words in Romans 15:13; it was his prayer for his friends in Rome. Three words stand out in this statement—hope, joy, and peace.

Paul tells us that our God is the God of hope. God wants us to look ahead with hope and not with despair. Whenever the Old Testament prophets thundered out their predictions of judgment, they always wove into the dark cloud of judgment the silver lining of hope. In fact, some of the greatest promises of hope in the Bible are found in the midst of dark messages of judgment.

You and I need never fear the future. God knows and controls the future. He knows the end from the beginning; He is the Alpha and Omega, the first and the last. God is never surprised or caught off guard. No matter how confused things may be on earth, God is on the throne of heaven, calmly guiding the affairs of history.

God wants us to abound in hope. This means having our hearts filled with His hope, and guiding our lives on the basis of the wonderful future God has prepared for His own. To abound in hope means much more than believing the promises of God; it means being motivated by these promises. It means living today in the light of eternity, with our lives controlled by the future, not by the past. What a tragedy it is when people permit themselves to be controlled by the past—past regrets, past failures, and past sins. Give your past to Christ—let Him wash it away—and start living on the basis of the blessed hope that you have in Him.

Don't try to manufacture hope in your own strength. Let the Holy Spirit who lives within you generate the hope that you need. We "abound in hope through the power of the Holy Spirit." Yield to the Spirit, let Him take control of your heart and mind. Spend time reading the Word of God, and you will discover the Spirit of God filling your heart with a wonderful hope. Of course, if you don't know Jesus Christ as your Savior, you have no hope. Yield to Him and the gift of hope will be yours through the power of the Holy Spirit.

But hope is just one of the treasures God gives us when we trust in Him. He also gives us joy. "Now the God of hope fill you with all joy and peace in believing. . . ." Christian joy is not the same as happiness, although it can include happiness. Happiness so often depends on happenings. If things are going right with us, we are happy; if the situation changes, we become unhappy. Joy is much deeper than that. It is inward confidence and well-being that only the Holy Spirit can give. I have experienced the deepest joy while suffering the greatest pain. Joy is not created by circumstances on the outside; it is the result of conditions on the inside.

The joyful Christian faces life without fear or complaint. Each new day is a new challenge. Each problem is an opportunity to grow and see God work. Joy is really a by-product of a life of service to God and others. If you start searching for joy, you will never find it. But if you surrender to God and do His will, joy will come to your heart. Joy adds a special quality to life that nothing else can add. Our friends can tell when this joy is overflowing in our hearts, and it is this kind of joy that attracts people to our Savior. Billy Sunday used to say, "If you have no joy in your religion, there's a leak in your Christianity somewhere."

Along with joy is the gift of peace. "Now the God of hope fill you with all joy and peace in believing. . . ." This is the peace that Jesus meant when He said to His followers, "Peace I leave with you; my peace I give unto you. Let not your heart be troubled, neither let it be afraid." Here was Jesus, facing the terrors of the cross, yet He was giving peace to His followers!

What a thrilling experience it is when you yield to the Spirit of God and let Him fill your heart with these gifts! With hope and joy and peace filling your heart, you can face life with a new power and courage, knowing that Christ will see you through.

The future is always bright because God has the future in His hands. For the Christian, the best is yet to come. Christ always saves the best wine for the last. For the unsaved person, the worst is yet to come. The unsaved man is having his heaven right now, because death is coming and after that the judgment. But the Christian never has to fear the future; his heart is filled with hope from the God of hope.

And the Christian never has to fret about the present, because his heart is filled with joy. No matter how difficult or uncomfortable the present circumstances might be, there is joy in our hearts from Jesus Christ. Paul wrote Philippians, his most joyful letter, while waiting to stand trial in Rome, knowing the possibility of his execution. Jesus talked about His joy while facing Calvary. "The joy of the Lord is your strength." You can live a day at a time, no matter how heavy the burdens may be, because you are filled with joy.

And, we never have to worry about the past because we have His peace. This is the "peace of God that passes all understanding. . . ." With God's peace filling our hearts, we are no longer haunted by past failures, mistakes, injuries, or even past sins. With Christ as our Savior the past is gone; God remembers it no more and holds it against us no more. We are completely and finally forgiven through Jesus Christ who died on the cross.

So, these three wonderful gifts take care of our past, present, and future. Whether we look back, look around, or look ahead, we need never be afraid. The God of hope fills us with all joy and peace in believing so that we abound in hope through the power of the Holy Spirit.

The key word here is *believing*. When we believe, God fills. Admit to God your worry about the past, your misery in the present, your frustration about the future. These are sins; confess them to God and let Him cleanse you. Then, by faith, ask Him to fill you with the Holy Spirit. You won't hear any bells ringing; you won't see any flashes of light; but you will experience within a deep sense of hope and peace and joy—three of God's treasures.

26

Put Joy into Your Life

Evangelist D. L. Moody encouraged Christian joy. He once said in a meeting, "There are too many religious meetings which are sadder than a funeral. They are a hindrance to the cause. They breed people with faces bearing an expression as chilling as an east wind from the lake." (Anyone who lives in Chicago, as Mr. Moody did, knows what he means by a cold east wind from off the lake!) What Mr. Moody says is true—the greatest obstacle to sinners coming to Christ is the joyless attitude of many professed Christians.

There is a difference between being serious and being solemn. God wants us to be serious, but I don't know of any place in the Bible where He commands us to be solemn, to have a long face and a miserable look that means death to all that are happy and joyful around us. A missionary executive once told me that he would never send a missionary to the field if the man or woman didn't have a sense of humor. To be able to laugh at yourself and at the world around you, and to be able to laugh with others, is a mark of maturity. A famous Shakespearean actress once said, "You grow up when you get your first laugh at yourself."

People who don't know how to laugh are usually bitter and critical and hard to live with. The man who can't laugh at his own mistakes has a hard time forgiving the mistakes of others. He harbors them down inside and they fester like an open sore. Nothing clears the air in a home or a church meeting like a good healthy laugh. I'm not talking about silly comedy; I'm talking about good healthy holy humor.

Jesus wants us to have joy. He had joy. He said to His disciples, "These things have I said unto you that your joy might be full." If the disciples had never seen Jesus smile or laugh, they would have wondered what kind of joy He was talking about. Yes, He was the man of sorrows; but He was also the man of joy. And the only way to have joy is to get it from Jesus Christ. You can go to the store and purchase fun, but you can't purchase joy. Jesus purchased it for you when He died for you on the cross.

Perhaps the greatest joy chapter in the Bible is Luke 15. There a woman finds her lost coin and rejoices; a shepherd finds his lost sheep and rejoices; and a father welcomes his lost son home and rejoices. And all of them invite their friends and neighbors to rejoice. Jesus says that even the angels in heaven rejoice when a sinner comes home and is forgiven. Certainly the sinner rejoices! The first step toward joy is to receive Christ as your Savior. When you do this, the Spirit of God moves into your life and "the fruit of the Spirit is love, joy, peace. . . ."

Christian people are joyful people. Their sins are forgiven. Their Father in heaven cares for them. They have a home waiting when this life is over. We can't always rejoice *over* our circumstances, but we can rejoice *in* our circumstances no matter how uncomfortable they may be. "Rejoice in the Lord always and again I say, rejoice."

Joy is the birthright of every believer. Knowing that you are saved, one of God's children, forgiven, going to heaven, is a source of endless joy. But some Christians seem to have lost that joy. Is this possible? And if it is, how can this joy be restored again?

One of the chief causes of a loss of joy is *sin, disobedience to God*. When David confessed his sins to God, he said, "Restore unto me the joy of thy salvation." David lost his joy, and for a year or more he lived under a dark cloud of despair and gloom. In Psalm 32 he tells us that he even suffered physically because of unconfessed sin. He became like an old sick man because his conscience was smiting him. So, if you have lost your joy in Christ, take inventory and see if perhaps there is unconfessed sin in your life.

A second thief that can rob us of joy is *neglecting the Word of God*. Jesus said, "These things I speak in the world, that they might have my joy fulfilled in themselves" (John 17:13). The prophet Jeremiah found joy in the Word of God. He said, "Thy words were found and I did eat them; and thy word was unto me the joy and rejoicing of mine heart" (Jer. 15:16). At the beginning of each day, I get alone with my Bible, and I read it. I ask God to speak to me, and He does. No matter how difficult my situation may be, God always has a promise or a commandment that gives me joy. Read the Bible if you want to increase your joy.

A third thief that will rob us of joy is *forgetting to pray*. Jesus said, "Ask, and ye shall receive, that your joy may be full" (John 16:24). If you and I depend on our own resources, we will be miserable, because our own resources are weak and limited. They run out just when we think we're over the top. But the resources of God never run out. God is the giver of every good and perfect gift, and His wealth can never fail. Prayer opens for you the treasury of God. "Ask and it shall be given unto you. . . . You have not because you ask not." If some problem is burdening you now, take time to pray about it; and God's joy will fill your heart again.

Don't let sin, neglect of the Bible, and prayerlessness rob you of your joy. God wants you to have joy. "The joy of the Lord is our strength." Joy lubricates the machinery of life and makes everything run much smoother. A joyful Christian is a strong Christian: Satan has a harder time tempting the man who has joy in his heart. A joyful Christian is a witnessing Christian because he has something exciting to share with others, and they can see the difference.

now let's talk about how to share your joy. If there are two commodities that are in short supply in our world today they are love and joy. Most of the people you and I meet during the day are hungry for love and joy. If you and I are filled with God's Spirit and walking in His power, then others will see love and joy in our lives. We won't have to manufacture them for the occasion; they will be fruit that are constantly growing and reproducing in our lives.

How do we share our joy? By our attitudes. We can't hide joy once it is in our hearts and running over! We don't have to wear signs telling people we are joyful! They will see it in our attitudes and actions. People watch us because we are Christians; and this gives us a wonderful opportunity to show them what a difference Christ has made in our lives. In fact, unsaved people might even create some problems for us just to see what we will do.

The joyful Christian also shares his joy by doing his job gladly and, not complaining about it. He tries his best not to add to anybody's problems. He is a part of the answer, not a part of the problem. He avoids criticizing others. He speaks the truth in love. The joyful Christian shares his joy by accepting the burdens of life without complaining. He is willing to do the small tasks that others ignore; and when he does the big jobs, he is willing for others to share the credit.

All around us are people who are lonely and bitter, and they need a good dose of Christian love and joy. They may not be the easiest people in the world to work with, eat with, or talk to; but they need what we have to offer. Let God lead you to them; ask God to help you understand their needs. Listen to what they say, even though you may disagree with some of it. Remember, you are not out to win an argument; you are out to win a soul to Christ. Your attitude of love and joy will soon take hold of his heart and this will give you an opportunity to share Christ with your friend.

Every hour of every day there is something to rejoice about, so start cultivating an attitude of joy. Keep your heart clean; spend time in the Word and prayer; look for ways to make life happier and easier for others. And when you do, a wonderful thing will happen to you: God's love and joy will fill your heart.

27

Divine Resources for Life's Difficulties

On October 31, 1517, Dr. Martin Luther nailed his ninety-five theses on the door of the church at Wittenberg, Germany. The result was what historians call the Reformation, an attempt to bring the truth of salvation by faith back to the hearts of the people. Out of the Reformation came a return, not only to biblical doctrine, but also to the singing of hymns in the churches. Martin Luther was an accomplished musician himself and he used music to express his faith and teach his people. "A Mighty Fortress Is Our God" is the one song more than any other that we associate with this great man and his work. Based on Psalm 46, this song has for centuries moved Christians to trust God no matter how difficult their circumstances might be.

In Psalm 46, we find three divine resources to sustain us in the difficulties of life. To begin with, we need not fear because we have a *refuge*. "God is our refuge and strength, a very present help in trouble. Therefore we will not fear. . . ." No matter what may happen to us, we can find refuge in the Lord. The psalmist also wrote, "Therefore will not we fear, though the earth be removed, and though the mountains be carried into the midst of the sea." The psalmist is saying, "Even if an earthquake occurs, I don't have to be afraid because God is my refuge and my strength." You see, my friend, nothing moves or changes God. God is not affected by the convulsions of society or the confusion of government. He is the rock—He stands secure—He will not be moved. When you and I run to Him for refuge, He is there to protect us.

But note that God is both our refuge *and* strength. We don't run to Him to hide; we run to Him for help. He hides us that He might help us, and then He thrusts us back into the battle that we might accomplish His will in this world. God does not hide us to pamper us, but to prepare us. He strengthens us that He might use us.

We have learned that we need not *fear* because we have a refuge; and Psalm 46 tells us that we need not *faint* because we have a river. "There is a river, the streams whereof shall make glad the city of God, the holy place of the tabernacles of the Most High. God is in the midst of her; she shall not be moved: God shall help her and that right early." Jerusalem is one great city that is not built on a river. The great Egyptian cities were built on the Nile; Babylon was built on the Euphrates; Rome is built by the Tiber. But Jerusalem had no river running through it for a water supply. Godly King Hezekiah built a marvelous water system for the city, bringing the water through the rock into Jerusalem. Archaeologists have discovered this system and you may walk through it in Jerusalem today.

Psalm 46 is not talking about a literal river, rather about the supply of spiritual power available from the Lord for His people. In the Bible, water for drinking is a picture of the Holy Spirit. In John 7, Jesus compares the Spirit of God to a river of living water. "If any man thirst, let him come unto me, and drink . . . and out of his belly shall flow rivers of living water. But this spake he of the Spirit. . . ."

No matter how difficult may be the problems of life, we need not fear because we have a refuge, and we need not faint because we have a river. God supplies us with the spiritual power we need to keep going in spite of the difficulties. "Not by might, nor by power, but by my Spirit, saith the

Lord of hosts." "But ye shall receive power when the Holy Spirit is come upon you. . . ." Of ourselves, we do not have the strength we need to keep going; but through the Holy Spirit, we can overcome. "I can do all things through Christ who strengthens me." Have you trusted Christ as your Savior? If you have, are you trusting Him for the power you need moment by moment and day by day? "As thy days, so shall thy strength be."

There is a third divine resource given to us in Psalm 46. We need not *fret* for we have a revelation: "Be still and know that I am God. The Lord of hosts is with us; the God of Jacob is our refuge." What a wonderful revelation—"Be still, and know that I am God."

The trouble with many of us is that we think we are God. We make our plans and pull strings and try to manipulate people and situations, only to discover that everything falls apart. "Be still and know. . . ." Know what? "That I am God." I Am is one of the great names of God. When Moses told God that it was impossible for him to obey God and lead Israel out of Egypt, God said to Moses, "Remember my name—I Am." Not "I would like to be" or "I hope to be," but I Am! I am God! And Moses went out in the power of God's name and defeated the enemy and set his people free.

Jesus picked up that same divine name when He was here on earth. " *I am* the bread of life. . . . *I am* the good shepherd. . . . *I am* the light of the world." Whatever you need, says Jesus, I Am. Man's name is I Am Not; we just don't have what it takes to make it alone. But God's name is I Am and His mighty resources are available to us.

When I was in seminary, my Hebrew professor told us that the words "Be still" literally mean "Take your hands off!" "Take your hands off and know that I am God." You could even translate it "Relax and know that I am God." In other words, "Get your hands off the situation—stop playing God—and permit me to take over." Sometimes God has to wait for us to make a real mess of things before we give up and let Him take over. Don't wait that long; take your hands off now and let God have His way.

Here, then, are three wonderful divine resources for you to draw upon in the difficult times of life. We need not fear; we have a refuge. We need not faint; we have a river. And we need not fret; we have a revelation: "Be still, and know that I am God." A mighty fortress is our God—a bulwark never failing!

28

Wealth that Really Counts

The late J. Paul Getty was reputed to be the richest man in the world. He once complained to a newspaper reporter that inflation was hurting him and that a billion dollars was not what it used to be! You and I probably would not know what to do with a billion dollars, and I doubt if that much money would make a Christian happier or holier. Because we know Jesus Christ as our Savior, we are the wealthiest people in the world. Ephesians 1:3 informs us that we Christians have been "blessed with all spiritual blessings in heavenly places in Christ."

When Paul wrote his letter to the Ephesian believers, he was addressing people who knew something about wealth. Ephesus was a wealthy city. It possessed one of the seven wonders of the ancient world, the great temple of Diana; and the temple itself was a bank where citizens deposited their valuables. Thousands of tourists came to Ephesus each year to see the temple of Diana, and of course, there was a brisk trade in selling souvenirs.

But there were some people in Ephesus who were rich beyond measure. They did not have great stores of gold or silver hidden away. They had something better than that— they had wealth beyond measure that could never be taken from them! Paul mentioned this wealth in the beginning of his Ephesian letter: "Blessed be the God and Father of our Lord

Jesus Christ who hath blessed us with all spiritual blessings in heavenly places in Christ.''

If you know Christ as your Savior, then this wealth belongs to you. You did not earn it; you do not deserve it. The wealth is yours only because of the grace of God as revealed in Jesus Christ. Paul puts it another way in his second letter to the church at Corinth: ''For you know the grace of our Lord Jesus Christ, that, though He was rich, yet for your sakes He became poor, that you through His poverty might be rich.'' What kind of wealth is this? Unless we can answer that question, our wealth can do us no good! Perhaps the best way to understand this wealth is to contrast it with the kind of wealth God gave Israel when they entered the Promised Land.

To begin with, *Israel's wealth was material; our wealth is spiritual.* God promised them a land flowing with milk and honey, a land with precious metals *in* the ground and wonderful crops *on* the ground. He promised them abundant harvests and growing flocks and herds. He promised them rain when they needed it, and He even told them that they would not suffer from the diseases they saw in the land of Egypt. Truly God gave Israel tremendous wealth.

Nowhere in the New Testament does God promise to make Christians wealthy and comfortable in this world. Jesus Himself was poor, and so were His disciples. Paul described himself as ''poor yet making many rich.'' Peter confessed, ''Silver and gold have I none.''

There is a brand of teaching in some places today that equates wealth with spirituality and God's blessing. If you are really a dedicated Christian, they say, then you will be traveling first-class with a big salary, a fancy house, and no sickness or worries or bills. I don't find this teaching in my Bible as far as the New Testament Christians are concerned.

Our wealth is spiritual. We have the ''blessings of the Spirit.'' These blessings mean much more than the material things of life. God has promised to meet all our needs, and

He has given us all the spiritual blessings necessary to live for Him and to glorify His name. Let's not measure life or spiritual stature by material things. Let's ask ourselves how many blessings of the Spirit we are really enjoying and investing in our lives.

There is a second contrast between the blessings God gave Israel and the blessings we have as believers in Jesus Christ: *their blessings were earthly, while ours are heavenly.* God promised to bless their crops, their flocks, their herds, their families, their armies, and even their rainfall. He promised them "days of heaven upon earth" and freedom from famine, sickness, and trouble. All of these are blessings that are attached to this world and the material things in it.

But the blessings we have in Christ are "in heavenly places." Right now, Jesus Christ is seated in heaven. According to Ephesians 2:6, you and I as believers are seated with Him and in Him. We may be on earth physically, but spiritually we are in heavenly places with Christ.

Let me illustrate this truth in a simple way. Have you ever been in love? Or have you ever watched somebody who is in love? When a person is in love, everything he says and does relates to the person he loves. No matter where he is physically, his heart and mind are with the one he loves; and this helps to control his life.

You and I are in heavenly places, and this means that our life on earth should be controlled by heaven. We are above the world. We are seated with Christ in the throne of the universe! What a privilege, and what a responsibility! This is what Paul writes, "Since then you are risen with Christ, seek those things which are above, where Christ sitteth on the right hand of God. Set your affection on things above and not on things on the earth." Our wealth is in the heavenlies, and our heart and mind should be there, too.

There is a third contrast between our wealth and the wealth God gave Israel in their land. *Our wealth is permanent and free, not temporary and conditional.* The Jews were blessed in their land as long as they obeyed God. But if they disobeyed Him, God might turn off the rain, dry up the rivers, blast the crops, and bring physical and economic disaster to the land. As you read your Old Testament, you find several occasions when the Lord disciplined His people by permitting famines and pestilences and even wars to come. Their blessings were temporary and conditional.

But our spiritual blessings in Christ are permanent and free. There are no strings attached! Our blessings are based on grace, not law. When you were saved, God blessed you with all the blessings of the Spirit you will ever need to live a full life and glorify His name. We are complete in Christ; nothing needs to be added, and nothing will be taken away.

But *enjoyment* of these blessings is conditional: we must yield to the Lord, trust Him, and by faith draw upon this vast spiritual wealth. A disobedient Christian is like the prodigal son: he has plenty of wealth and satisfaction with his father back home, but he can never enjoy it in the pigpen! God will never take away our blessings in Christ, but we by our unbelief or disobedience can rob ourselves of the enjoyment of these blessings.

You were born rich when you were born again through faith in Christ. If you and I major on the spiritual blessings, you can be sure God will take care of the material blessings and mercies for us. Read your Bible and discover how rich you are in Christ. Then kneel in prayer and ask God to help you appropriate these blessings by faith. There is no need to live like a pauper when you can live like a king!

29

Give Me this Mountain

Every nation has its forgotten heroes, and this is true of Old Testament history as well. We readily think of men like Abraham, Isaac, Jacob, Joseph, Moses, or David. But how often do we hear about a man named Caleb? When Caleb was eighty-five years old, he came to Joshua to claim his inheritance in the Promised Land. He said, "Now therefore give me this mountain." What an example Caleb is for us today!

When the nation of Israel neared the Promised Land, Moses sent twelve men into the land to spy it out. The men came back with a glowing report of the riches in the land and even brought samples of the fruit. They had clusters of grapes so large that it took two men to carry them. But, sad to say, ten of the twelve men had absolutely no faith that God could give them the land. They saw only the walled cities and the giants who lived in them. However, two of the spies, Joshua and Caleb, tried to convince the people that God was able to give them victory, but alas, the majority ruled, and the nation turned back into the wilderness. They wandered for forty years, until all of that unbelieving generation died—except Moses and Joshua and Caleb.

God did lead His people into the Promised Land. Joshua led them across the Jordan River and into the land, and they won victory after victory. Then it came time for the people to claim their share of the inheritance, and that was when Caleb said, "Give me this mountain." Caleb didn't ask for an easy place; he asked for a difficult place. The Bible tells us that this mountain was inhabited by a race of giants who lived in walled cities; but these obstacles didn't stop Caleb. He asked for the mountain, and by faith in God, he claimed that mountain and gave it to his family for generations to come.

What are some of the lessons we learn from this forgotten hero, Caleb? For one thing, we learn that *the defeats of others need not make us losers as well*. Because of the unbelief of the ten spies and the rest of Israel, Caleb had to wander in the wilderness for forty years, when he could have been enjoying his inheritance. But Caleb didn't give up just because the majority was wrong. Caleb continued to trust God, knowing that one day he would claim his inheritance.

Perhaps you are suffering because of another's mistakes or sins. Look at Caleb and learn the importance of trusting God in spite of what others do. Like Caleb, we can afford to wait, knowing that one day God is going to honor our faith and give us our inheritance. Caleb's body may have been in the wilderness, but his heart was in the Promised Land. Isn't that the way we Christians should live? Our citizenship is in heaven—our hearts ought to be in heaven. Keep trusting the Lord; your inheritance is secure with Him.

The more I think about Caleb, that mighty Old Testament hero, the more I appreciate him. He was certainly a man of faith: though the rest of the nation doubted God, Caleb believed God and was sure that one day he would get his promised reward. But there is a second lesson he teaches us: *age is no barrier to making conquests for the Lord*. Here was a man eight-five years old! And he is asking for a mountain! Not just any mountain, but a mountain controlled by a tribe of great and mighty warriors. Eight-five is a good age to settle down in some comfortable valley, but Caleb asked for a mountain.

If the years are adding up and you think your work is

done, dismiss that idea from your mind. These were not declining years for Caleb; they were years of going higher! He wanted to live in the mountain! How important it is to have an optimistic, enthusiastic attitude toward life. Caleb didn't say that his best years were over; he said that his best years were yet to come.

Granted, Caleb was still in good health; and this means a lot. But Caleb's power came from his faith in God. He knew that God was able to overcome the enemy and give him his inheritance. "And this is the victory that overcomes . . . even our faith." To complain is to sin; to worry is to sin; but to trust God for the future and claim His inheritance is to enter into a life of joy and satisfaction.

I don't know what mountains you may be facing just now. Perhaps there is a mountain of debt before you—medical bills or some other obligation. Perhaps it is a mountain of suffering, or you may be facing surgery. Don't look upon that mountain as an enemy to shun: look upon it as an inheritance to claim. Ask God to give you that mountain, and trust Him to see you through to victory.

Caleb is a man who teaches us *to look ahead and not back*. When the nation of Israel finally did enter the Promised Land, Caleb could have sat down and pouted. He could have reminded the rulers that he had been in the minority—he had voted to enter the land—and had been right. He could have reviewed those forty years of wasted wandering and complained about them. But he didn't! Instead of looking back, Caleb looked ahead and claimed his mountain.

There is some value in looking back. Moses told the people to remember the way God had led them, and he warned them not to forget what God had done for them. In the Lord's Supper we look back to remember Christ and His death for us on the cross. But we also look ahead to the time when Christ will come again for His people. No, looking back in itself is not a sin. But when looking back keeps us from looking ahead, then we are disobeying God.

Caleb didn't look back. He looked ahead and trusted God to give him a victorious future. Caleb's motto was, "The best is yet to come!" And isn't that the motto of every true Christian? There are always new blessings to receive, new lessons to learn, new victories to win. Life would be terribly boring if God didn't bring new challenges to our lives from time to time.

The beautiful thing about Caleb's victory is that he was able to leave that mountain inheritance to his family. His children and grandchildren enjoyed that mountain in the years that followed. The decisions we make in life affect other people. If we run from the challenges of life, then we lose that inheritance to leave to others. But if, like Caleb, we face the challenges honestly and claim them by faith, then we enrich our inheritance, and this means blessings to others.

Whenever I think of Caleb, I think of Jesus Christ. He faced a mountain one day called Calvary. It was on Calvary that Jesus would die for the sins of the world and thereby claim the greatest inheritance in history. He would make it possible for sinners to become the children of God and enter into heaven. He would leave behind for us a magnificent inheritance. The apostle Peter tells us that this inheritance is "incorruptible, and undefiled and fades not away." Caleb had to fight many battles against the giants to claim his inheritance. Jesus fought one battle on Calvary, and gave His life to secure the victory; and now He reigns as King of Kings and Lord of Lords, and we reign with Him as we yield ourselves to Him.

If you want to claim your mountain, begin by surrendering to Christ. He alone can give you the faith and courage to face life and conquer the enemy.

30

Contentment—Where?

Do your circumstances bother you? Are you at that place in life where you wish nothing would change, and yet everything is changing? Are you having to adjust to new surroundings or new people? Then Paul has a good word for you: "For I have learned, in whatsoever state I am, therewith to be content" (Phil. 4:11).

It is a great mistake to build your happiness on circumstances or things, because circumstances change and things have a way of wearing out and losing their value. True internal peace cannot be based on changing external things. We need something deeper and more satisfying.

Yet, most people build their happiness on the passing, external things of this world. And, for this reason, they are never really happy. Recently, I chatted with a lady who could only say, "Oh, I'd give anything if my husband were back again!" She and I both know that he is not going to come back again, and she also knows that it is foolish to build her life on a day-dream.

Real contentment must come from within. You and I cannot change or control the world *around* us, but we can change and control the world *within* us. It has often been said that what life does *to* us depends on what life finds *in* us. This explains Paul's great testimony, "For I have learned, in whatsoever state I am, therewith to be content."

The word *content* does not mean "complacent." Paul was anything but complacent! He felt the burden of lost souls and carried the gospel to city after city regardless of peril or persecution. Nor is contentment a dreamy attitude or vague feelings that lift you out of the world and make you immune to trouble and trial. Some people are always looking for new ways to be immunized against the hurts of life or protected from the bumps and scars of life. This is not contentment.

Actually, the word Paul used is best translated "contained." It carries the idea of self-sufficiency. In other words, Paul is saying, "I don't depend on things on the outside, because I carry my own sufficiency on the inside." This inner sufficiency, of course, is the power of Jesus Christ in Paul's life, for he goes on to say, "I can do all things through Christ who strengthens me."

Contentment, then, is actually *containment*—having the spiritual resources within to face life courageously and handle it successfully. Contentment is divine adequacy. Contentment is having that spiritual artesian well within so that you don't have to run to the broken cisterns of the world to get what you need. The power of Christ in the inner man is all we need for the demands of life. Resources on the outside, such as friends and counselors and encouragements, are only helpful as they strengthen our resources on the inside.

If you had all the props and crutches taken away from your life, would you be able to stand? Do you have that divine sufficiency and adequacy within? You can have it if you are willing to let God have His way.

How did Paul reach his high level of Christian experience? He tells us, "I have *learned*. . . ." It was not a natural gift that came automatically with his salvation. It was something that Paul learned, and the word means, "learned by experience."

This is where you and I usually fall down. We want to receive inner contentment and spiritual adequacy instantly by reading a book, or praying a prayer, or perhaps listening to a sermon, but that is not the way we become adequate in the inner man. We learn it by experience. This means we must go through troubles and trials, difficulties and sacrifices, and we must face changes in our lives. If everything remains the same, then we will die of the *status quo*. Life will become a comfortable coffin; but who wants to be a comfortable corpse?

Resistance to change is one of the chief causes of discontent and worry. We want to keep ourselves, our children, and our lives just as they are. We fight change, and in so doing, we rob ourselves of the contentment God can give us if we will but yield to Him. My widow friend for years has been rebelling against the painful reality that her husband is dead. Her rebellion will not bring him back, but it is protecting her from the necessity of accepting changes in her life. Her daydreams are cushions that keep her from being hurt by reality. But they are also substitutes that are keeping her from growing up.

There is not growth without challenge, and there is no challenge without change. If our lives are going to be isolated and insulated we will never face any challenges, but this means we will never have opportunities to mature. For mature people, life is a battleground, but they are willing to face the battles and, by faith, win the victories. For immature people, life is a playground; and they want to avoid battles, but this means they never have the joy of winning victories and growing in the Lord.

Read II Corinthians 11 and 12 if you want to see what kind of lessons and examinations Paul had in the school of life! "In stripes above measure. . . . [he was beaten] in prisons more frequent, in deaths often. . . . Three times I was beaten with rods, once was I stoned, three times I suffered shipwreck, a night and a day have I been in the deep. . . ." And add to these the dangers that he faced in his many travels, the opposition of the enemy, and the burden of caring for all the churches, and you can see that life was not gentle toward

Paul. He served "in weariness and painfulness, in hunger and thirst . . . in cold and nakedness. . . ."

But did Paul sit down and feel sorry for himself? No! Did he resign his calling and look for a place to retire? No! Instead of giving up, Paul *looked up* and asked God for the grace he needed to live for Christ and accomplish God's will. God said, "My grace is sufficient for thee." Paul discovered the inner resources of the Holy Spirit, the same resources that you and I must discover if we are to be content. Paul learned by difficult experience how to be a self-contained man, how to carry within him all the resources he needed to live for Christ.

Those difficulties that you are fighting, and about which you are complaining, may be the very tools God wants to use to give you inner peace and sufficiency. Stop fighting—yield to Christ—and you too will learn how to be content.

Whenever I read Paul's Letter to the Philippians, I have to remind myself that it was written from a Roman prison. Paul was a prisoner in Rome, chained twenty-four hours a day to a Roman soldier, and facing possible execution. Yet this letter is saturated with joy. Some eighteen times in this little letter Paul uses the words *joy* or *rejoice*. Paul knew that real joy does not come from comfortable circumstances on the outside, but from spiritual adequacy on the inside. Whether Paul was in prison or in a palace, whether he was with friends or with enemies, he had an inner sufficiency from Christ that carried him through.

How does this inner contentment reveal itself? To begin with, we have a peace that keeps us from falling apart and doing impulsive things. We have a patience that sustains us when all around us seems to be disintegrating. There is an inner peace and poise that makes us master of the situation—victors, not victims. We are able to look the situation right in the eye, face it honestly and deal with it intelligently and courageously.

Read Acts 27 and see Paul's sufficiency on board ship in

the midst of the storm. Paul went on that ship as a prisoner, but before long, he was the master of the ship! When others had given up, Paul announced that God would spare their lives. He could say, "Wherefore, sirs, be of good cheer: for I believe God. . . ." Paul had learned by experience how to be adequate through Christ for any situation of life.

This secret is not for apostles only; it is for any Christian who will learn it. Listen again to Paul's inspired testimony: "I have learned the secret of being content, no matter what situation I am in. . . . I can do all things through Christ who strengthens me."

Why Us? When bad things happen to God's people

WARREN W. WIERSBE

Pain or disaster often descend suddenly from a clear blue sky. At first we are stunned. Then we start asking questions,

'What does it mean?'
'Doesn't God *care*?'
'Why me?'
'Why us?'

Warren Wiersbe handles these questions with clarity, compassion and biblical wisdom. He shows that God is an ever-present source of comfort, strength and hope, even if he seems a million miles away. Through faith we can survive life's bad weather, even bolts from the blue.

'Sensitively written, logical, rooted in the Scriptures . . .'
Charles W. Colson, Founder, Prison Fellowship.

160 pages   Pocketbook

Inter-Varsity Press

Does God Answer?

CARROLL E. SIMCOX

'O my God, I cry out to you, but you do not answer . . .'
This ancient cry of despair has a modern ring to it. Does God really answer prayer? Do we just pretend that he does?

Carroll Simcox believes that all prayers are answered and in this book explores, with uncommon insight, how it happens.

Along the way he exposes many of our foibles and misconceptions about prayer, ourselves and God. Even though our best prayers are little better than childish prattle, God transforms them into the language of heaven.

114 pages   Pocketbook

Inter-Varsity Press

The Fight

JOHN WHITE

John White has written this book because he wants you to understand clearly what the Christian life is all about. He wants you to learn in the depths of your being that the eternal God loves you and plans only your highest good – more trust in him, more likeness to him.

But his love will bring pain as intense as your joy. For the Christian life is a fight. . . .

"Reading *The Fight* is to inhale great draughts of fresh air into one's Christian life . . . This is the kind of book every 20th Century Christian should have on his book shelf."

Church of England Newspaper

230 pages   Pocketbook

Inter-Varsity Press

Take my life

MICHAEL GRIFFITHS

It's an all-or-nothing, round-the-clock commitment. Following Jesus means unconditional obedience, sacrificial service, and total devotion to God's will.

Michael Griffiths shows us what the Bible says about serving the Lord with all our will, time, and money; all our mind and love; all that we do or say, and all that we are.

190 pages   Pocketbook

Inter-Varsity Press

Know the truth

BRUCE MILNE

'You will know the truth,' said Jesus, 'and the truth will set you free.'

Christians have already begun to know God and his truth. This handbook will help us to grow in that liberating knowledge, as it opens up the great themes of God's Word and shows us how they fit together.

Each chapter looks at one facet of biblical truth and encourages further study with Scripture references to look up, questions for discussion and books for additional reading. The main sections all close with practical reflection on how the Bible's teaching challenges us and moves us to adore the living God.

288 pages   Large paperback

Inter-Varsity Press